Green Line

Kevin McCormack

Ian Allan PUBLISHING

Contents

This is a postwar view of a 6Q6, captioned 'Henry and Peter Jones at Hertford'. *Author's collection*

Front cover:
The enduring memory of Green Line operations in the 1950s and 1960s is epitomised in this view of modernised RF208 heading north towards Mickleham near the Burford Bridge Hotel at the foot of Box Hill. This idyllic scene dates from May 1969. *Mike Harries*

Back cover:
Bringing the Green Line story right up to date is No 4364, a Plaxton-bodied DAF SB 3000, delivered new to ARRIVA The Shires in July 2000 for use on the prestigious 757 service. This view was taken at Hyde Park Corner on 11 September 2000. *Geoff Rixon*

Title page:
The London Transport fleetname has been applied to T680, which otherwise is in full Green Line regalia on this route 725 working in Kingston. On the left is TD42 and, in the background, an RTW waiting to return to Putney Bridge on the 85 service. T680 served as a US forces 'Clubmobile' canteen named 'Milwaukee' during the war. *Geoff Rixon*

First published 2000

ISBN 0 7110 2738 2

Published by Ian Allan Publishing
an imprint of Ian Allan Publishing Ltd,
Terminal House, Shepperton, Surrey TW17 8AS.

Printed by Ian Allan Printing Ltd,
Riverdene Business Park, Hersham, Surrey KT12 4RG.

Code: **0010/B2**

Introduction

With the 70th anniversary of Green Line's creation occurring on 9 July 2000, it seemed appropriate to mark the occasion with a book covering the history of this famous express coach network, which at one time sped through virtually the whole of the former London Transport (LT) operating area within roughly a 30-mile radius of the capital. The Green Line which enters the new millennium is a very different type of operation, having been adapted to suit current passenger needs and traffic conditions. The old cross-London network and most of the former routes have gone, but a smaller and increasing number of Green Line services still bring passengers into the capital, or to some of London's airports, from most points of the compass within the Home Counties.

My earliest recollections of Green Line coach travel go back to the start of the 1950s and are far from happy. At the time, my parents were house-hunting in the Purley area, and we used to travel long distances by Green Line. I was not a good traveller, except in surface trains. I could survive short, bumpy bus journeys if there was plenty of ventilation: the older the vehicle, the better. But I could not cope with the smoothness of the Green Line vehicles (new RFs, presumably) and would turn greener than the paintwork of the coaches after a comparatively short time. I recall one occasion, after a particularly bad journey, when my parents tried to cheer me up by taking me to a toy shop in Caterham to buy something. What did I choose? A clockwork LT-style trolleybus — a clear case of being hooked at an early age!

At the time of Green Line's Golden Jubilee there was much celebration, and three definitive works were published in 1980: books by A. McCall (New Cavendish), Kenneth Warren (Ian Allan) and D. W. K. Jones & H. J. Davis (London Country). These books have provided me with much of the material for this *Glory Days* volume. In addition, *History of 'East Surrey'* by 'Bell Street' (HJ Publications), Ken Glazier's *RF* and *The Last Years of the General* (Capital Transport), and Gavin Martin's *London Buses 1929-1939* (Ian Allan) have also proved useful. Information covering the last 20 years has been gleaned from various magazine articles etc, and I have been very fortunate to have had the kind assistance of Clive King, Managing Director of Green Line Travel Ltd, now an ARRIVA company.

I am most grateful to the many contributors who have provided material, whether their own or from their collections, without which this book would not have been produced. I have tried, wherever possible, to select photographs which will not be familiar to readers, and I owe a particular debt to John Aldridge for the rare, early material from his collection. In addition, special thanks goes to the ever youthful (and useful!) Geoff Rixon, whose photographs in this book span over 50 years, and who is still pedalling furiously in and around London regularly, carrying his camera. This book also features work by Maurice Bateman, Michael Furnell, Steve Fennell, Gerald Mead, the late Mike Harries, Vernon Murphy, Peter Plummer, Derek Parsons, Mike Pope, Albert Dunkley, C. Carter, Ron Stevens, Trevor Puttock and Max Hayles, to whom I am most grateful. Finally, I should like to extend my appreciation to Tony Beard, Dave Churn, Jef Johnson, John Gilmartin and Trevor Saunders, for their valuable help in various ways.

We are very fortunate to have a considerable legacy of former Green Line vehicles in preservation. The largest and rarest collections can be found at Cobham Bus Museum, near Weybridge, in Surrey and in the London Transport Collection at Covent Garden and Acton. There are also large numbers of individually-owned vehicles not kept in museums — particularly RFs, and a few RT and Routemaster coaches, as well as various more modern representatives. A few still remain in regular service, eg with Stagecoach East London, and Nostalgiabus of Mitcham.

There is a great deal of affection and respect for the Green Line 'brand-name' and its historic associations. I hope that readers will enjoy this book, which seeks to bring together Green Line's illustrious past, its darker times and its promising future.

Kevin R. McCormack
Ashtead, Surrey
July 2000

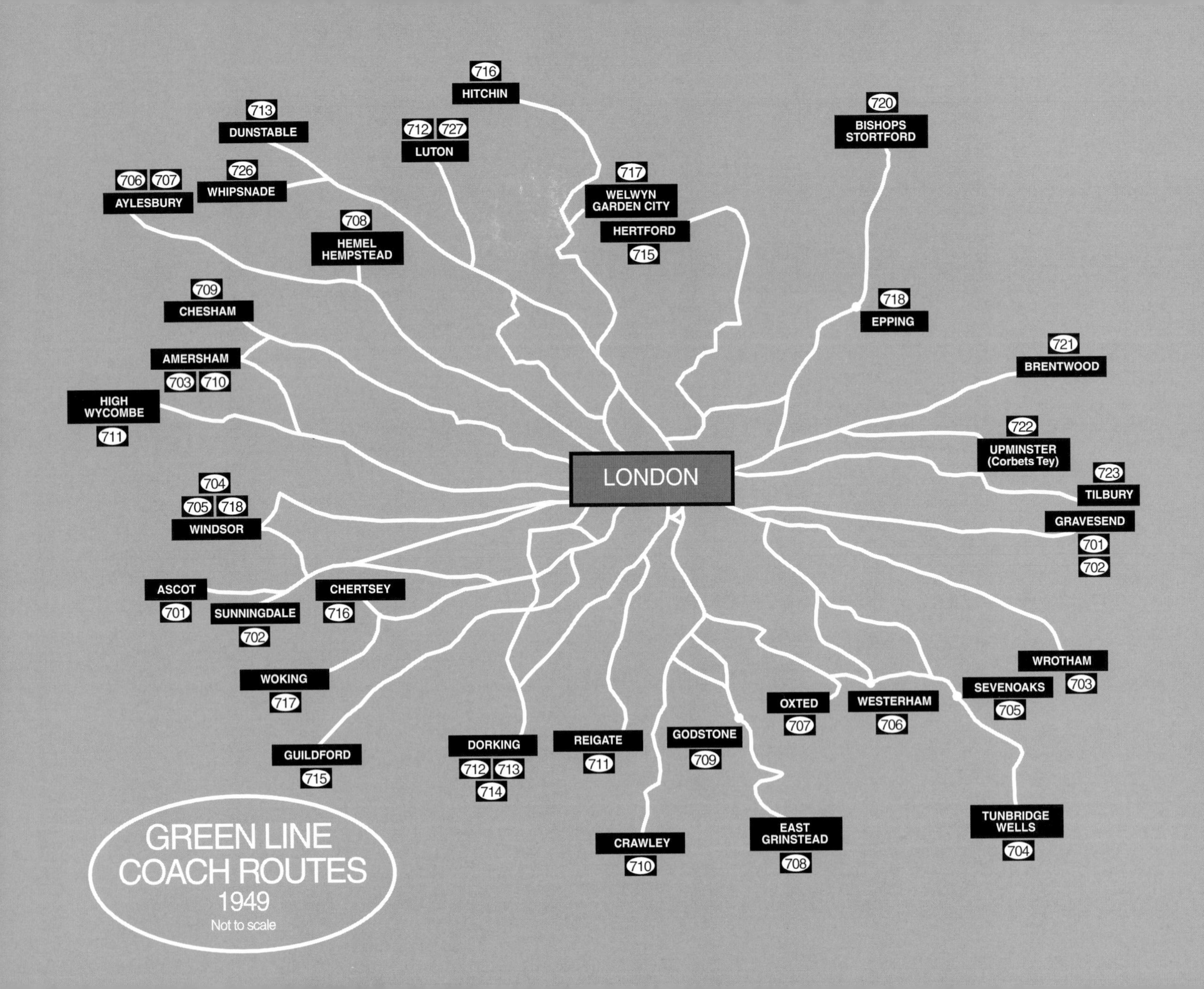
716
HITCHIN
713
DUNSTABLE
712 727
LUTON
720
BISHOPS STORTFORD
726
WHIPSNADE
706 707
AYLESBURY
717
WELWYN GARDEN CITY
HERTFORD
715
708
HEMEL HEMPSTEAD
709
CHESHAM
718
EPPING
721
BRENTWOOD
AMERSHAM
703 710
HIGH WYCOMBE
711
722
UPMINSTER (Corbets Tey)
LONDON
723
TILBURY
704
705 718
WINDSOR
GRAVESEND
701
702
ASCOT
701
SUNNINGDALE
702
CHERTSEY
716
WOKING
717
WROTHAM
703
SEVENOAKS
705
OXTED
707
WESTERHAM
706
GODSTONE
709
REIGATE
711
DORKING
712 713
714
GUILDFORD
715
CRAWLEY
710
EAST GRINSTEAD
708
TUNBRIDGE WELLS
704
GREEN LINE COACH ROUTES
1949
Not to scale

◂◂ Map of Green Line routes, 1949.

◂ Former second-series 7T7 T232 poses outside Weymann's at Addlestone in April 1933, carrying its unique all-metal body. *John Aldridge collection*

A first-series (7T7) T-type, complete with curtains, waits at Bush House, Aldwych on the inaugural Green Line coach service which started on 17 July 1930. T134 was sold by LT in August 1938.
John Aldridge collection

Green Line — The Early Days (1930-1945)

The origin of Green Line services lay with the London General Omnibus Company (LGOC), a subsidiary of the Underground Electric Railway Company. LGOC was becoming increasingly concerned at the upsurge of short-distance express-coach services into London in the late 1920s. The operators of these services were exploiting a loophole in the legislation which enabled their vehicles to stop and pick up passengers in the LGOC area. Fearful of losing traffic from its bus routes, LGOC set up its own Express Coach department in 1929 with the intention of running coach services in direct competition with other operators and forcing them out of business.

The first route was from Watford to Golders Green, connecting with the Underground, which started on 2 October 1929. Strangely, the service was withdrawn on 12 November 1929, but was reinstated on 18 December 1929, concurrently with the introduction of a second service, from Watford through to Charing Cross.

The inauguration of new express-coach services which were subsequently linked to Green Line is difficult to chronicle because, for the first two years or so, the services were in the hands of several operators. Strictly speaking, East Surrey had started the ball rolling by running an express service from 7 August 1928 between Reigate/Redhill and Northumberland Avenue (near Charing Cross/Trafalgar Square). At that time, East Surrey was both an operating agent for LGOC and an operator in its own right. This coach service, however, was an East Surrey initiative, masterminded by the company's dynamic Managing Director, Arthur Hawkins. Yet, on this occasion, Mr Hawkins was somewhat ahead of his time, because the service ceased on 2 March 1929 due to insufficient demand. It was to be over a year before East Surrey had another attempt at entering the express-coach market.

The two LGOC services from Watford were started with spare coaches from the Private Hire fleet which were not

Two first-series 7T7s stand in Poland Street Coach Station, which opened for service on Christmas Day, 1930. The bill-board propped up against the waiting room advertises 'Guildford by Green Line'. The Guildford service was one of the first two to use this terminus which was off Oxford Street. T144 carries a Short Bros body and was withdrawn by LT in December 1938. *John Aldridge collection*

required over the winter months. These were AEC Reliances with folding roofs, painted light green and cream. Clearly, if LGOC was to expand these operations, it urgently needed a fleet of purpose-built coaches. LGOC had already ordered 50 single-deck AEC Regal buses, numbered T1-50, and these entered service from December 1929. However, T38 was held back and, when it emerged in March 1930, it had undergone considerable modification. The floor was raised so that the seats all faced forward and were all at the same height, including those positioned over the rear wheel-arches. This made the vehicle look taller, because the windows were set higher. Folding doors were fitted at the top of the stairs leading up from the rear entrance, and the seating was upgraded and less cramped.

T38 entered service on 1 April 1930 at Watford (Leavesden Road), operating on the Golders Green express service. In the meantime, an order had been placed in February 1930 for 100 similar 27-seat coaches and, in order to accelerate delivery, only 50 of the bodies were constructed by LGOC, the remainder being contracted-out to Hall Lewis and Shorts. These vehicles were numbered T51-149 and T155 and, with their decorative curtains, luggage racks, heaters and route-points (place-names) painted on to the window louvres, the coaches looked quite different from the bus series. The first 40 of the class were painted in the LGOC colours of red and black with light grey roof. A further 26 carried the same livery, but with East Surrey or Autocar fleetnames. The remainder, starting with T119, were delivered in Green Line livery. By the end of the year, five of the class, which was now being augmented by a further 50 vehicles (T157-206), had been repainted into Amersham & District colours, this company having come under LGOC control, like East Surrey and Autocar. The gap in the number series arose because T150-154 were private hire coaches for LGOC and T156 was a Central Area bus to replace T38.

To return to LGOC operations, the next service to be introduced was from Windsor to Charing Cross (Embankment) via Slough and Hammersmith. This started on 20 April 1930 using the new red-and-black-liveried T-type Regals which, by this time, had replaced the Reliances on the two Watford services. The following month, red and black T-class Regals reached East Surrey and Autocar for new services to Oxford Circus starting on 6 June 1930. Three of these services were East Surrey's: from Dorking via Epsom, Redhill via Croydon and Reigate via Sutton; the fourth was Autocar's, from Tunbridge Wells.

On 10 July 1930, LGOC introduced a new Windsor service to Charing Cross (Embankment) via Staines and Hounslow but, in the context of this book, this was overshadowed by an event which occurred on the previous day. LGOC was becoming increasingly concerned about the apparent difficulty the public was experiencing in distinguishing the new express coaches from their normal buses, which then raised problems over the absence, at this time, of one-penny (1d) fares. The solution was to form a new LGOC subsidiary with a separate identity and its own distinctive livery. So it was that on 9 July 1930, Green Line Coaches Ltd was registered, along with three other companies, Red Line, Blue Line and Yellow Line. These never traded but were set up for name protection purposes.

Eight days later, on 17 July 1930, the first Green Line route was inaugurated: Guildford to Charing Cross via the Kingston bypass. Also on the same date, Green Line took over the two Watford services using T-class coaches carrying the new fleetname. After that, there was a spread of new routes using the various LGOC names: Green Line, General, East Surrey, Autocar and National, the latter being another LGOC subsidiary operating on an agency basis like East Surrey, but concentrated in the north west of the area. Most coaches carried the Green Line fleetname, but

▲ ◄◄ These scenes, taken at Aylesbury (Market Square) in October 1931 and the London Terminal Coach Station in March 1932, show Premier Line and Blue Belle services. Premier Line was acquired by LPTB on 20 December 1933 along with 39 Leyland coaches. Blue Belle's East Grinstead service was taken over by Green Line on 20 July 1932, along with six AEC Regals. *John Aldridge collection*

◄ With 26 routes to operate in 1931, Green Line often had to rely on borrowed vehicles for relief work. This December 1931 view, taken in the brand-new Reigate garage, depicts one of East Surrey's six AEC Regal Private Hire coaches (C28R) with Hall Lewis 'all-weather' bodies (ie with fold-back canvas roof). On transfer to LGCS, these vehicles became Nos T309-314. *John Aldridge collection*

On 1 July 1933 Green Line reached Gravesend, and the existing Maidstone & District service was re-routed. M&D No 628, a Harrington-bodied Leyland Tiger identical to some acquired by LPTB, departs from Victoria Coach Station in April 1932.
John Aldridge collection

Out with the hunt in January 1934 is T265, a Ransomes-bodied second-series Regal which served as a staff ambulance during the war and then ran as a bus until March 1950. *John Aldridge collection*

LPTB acquired no fewer than 220 Gilfords, a type which was technically advanced and gave a particularly smooth ride by virtue of the Gruss air springs (see the mechanism on either side of the radiator). GF123 previously belonged to Hillman's Saloon Coaches. On 10 January 1934, LPTB took over the Bow to Brentwood section of Hillman's routes to Chelmsford and beyond, together with the garage at London Road, Romford.
John Aldridge collection

SEVENOAKS
GREEN LINE
GH 3823

Reigate garage contains a wide assortment of buses and coaches, mainly of East Surrey origin, in this July 1934 view. On the far left is Duple-bodied T260, which survived as a stores lorry (No 395w) until April 1960. Next to T260 is a first-series 7T7, an ex-M&D Gilford and an ex-Hillman Gilford. The vehicles against the back wall appear in close-up on page 91.
John Aldridge collection

for licensing, staffing and vehicle-ownership reasons it was not possible for all the routes to be operated at the outset by Green Line. However, from 1 October 1930, the transfer to Green Line of existing coach routes started to gain momentum, coinciding with the appearance of vehicles in Green Line's own livery of green and black. By the end of the year, the company was operating 24 coach routes, requiring 160 vehicles, with extras hired for peak periods.

Right from the outset, Green Line was aware that the proliferation of uncontrolled coach services by different operators was causing concern to the traffic authorities, which considered this to be a major cause of vehicle congestion in London. To pre-empt the inevitable legislation, Green Line introduced two measures. The first was to start linking up routes on either side of London to create through services, thus reducing roadside termini in the capital. This reorganisation started on 10 December 1930 with the creation of cross-London routes from Reigate to Welwyn Garden City and Great Bookham to Harpenden. The second measure was to create an off-street terminus near Oxford Street. Located in Broadwick Street, but referred to as Poland Street, the coach station, which could accommodate 12 vehicles, was opened on Christmas Day, 1930. Within three weeks, only four routes were still using the roadside terminus on the Embankment. Yet, despite its striking art deco frontage, Poland Street Coach Station was far from ideal operationally, due to the difficult access caused by the narrowness of the adjoining streets.

Coinciding with the opening of the Poland Street terminus was the entry into service of the first members of a second series of T-class Regal coaches, T207-306. These differed from the first series in having a front entrance and sliding door instead of a rear entrance and folding door. This design change reduced loading time and increased passenger capacity from 27 to 30 seats. In anticipation of legislation limiting the growth of new services, Green Line wasted no time in getting these vehicles on the road. All 100 coaches received bodies from outside contractors (Weymann, Ransomes and Duple) and were in service by February 1931. Green Line also took the opportunity

◄ The 50-strong 9T9 class, introduced in 1936, were stylish coaches but somewhat underpowered for Green Line operation, and fell from favour when the larger-engined 10T10s arrived two years later. Following the resumption of services after the war, the 9T9s were soon relegated to bus work, as illustrated here at Staines West station by Addlestone's T407. *Geoff Rixon*

at this time to take stock of its extraordinary growth in the first eight months of its existence by allocating letters from A to Z to all 26 routes then in operation.

The urgency for increasing the size of the fleet was prompted by legislation introducing nationwide licensing arrangements for bus and coach services. Those operating before 9 February 1931 were given 'established facility' status and received their licences, hence the rush to set up new routes before the deadline. After 9 February, new services would have to be justified and it became apparent that, in the London area, the regulations were being used to encourage local bus and railway services in preference to new coach services entering the capital. Rather than expanding, Green Line spent much of 1931 appealing against the refusal of the authorities to grant licences to the company. Expansion did restart from February 1932, but this was through Green Line's acquiring its competitors. In most cases, these companies initially kept their separate identities in order to protect the existing licences, although the services were included in the Green Line route-lettering system and were marketed by Green Line.

In the light of increasing hostility towards the licensing arrangements, restrictions on new coach operations were to some extent relaxed, but limitations were placed on the frequency of boarding points and the location of termini/stopping places in Central London. This resulted in the closure of Poland Street Coach Station on 3 October 1933, routes being transferred to Eccleston Bridge, Victoria, on the boundary of the restricted area. At the same time, a revised route-lettering system was

Ordered simultaneously with the 9T9 class were 50 Q-type coaches classified 6Q6. The above view, taken in early 1937, depicts Q195 picking up on Portsmouth Road, Esher, just short of the Scilly Isles roundabout. The bus shelter, manufactured by Astolat of Peasmarsh, near Guildford, expired 40 years later after a gale (see lower picture by Trevor Puttock), but an identical one still stands two stops further back near the entrance to Sandown Park. A brand-new one, of the same basic design but flat-backed, has recently been placed near the Queen's Stand on Epsom Downs, albeit not an Astolat product, because this firm closed down in January 1996.
John Aldridge collection

▲
▶

introduced on a clockwise basis, replacing the original haphazard lettering scheme. Most of the routes were by now operating across London, apart from the east and northeast services terminating at Aldgate.

The emergence on 1 July 1933 of the London Passenger Transport Board (LPTB), with its monopolistic powers to acquire the independent operators or their services inside the defined LPTB area (roughly within a 35-mile radius of London) brought an end to the three-year life of Green Line Coaches as an independent company and scotched any aspirations for reaching out further from London, eg to Oxford, Cambridge and the South Coast. It would be the 1980s before these ambitions were fulfilled. The LPTB takeover also meant the loss of Autocar, most of whose operations fell outside the designated territory. Autocar went to Maidstone & District but Green Line took over the Tunbridge Wells to Woking via London service, together with the associated coach station and garage at Tunbridge Wells. Green Line itself now became a trading name within the LPTB's Country Bus & Coach Department. But along with Green Line Coaches Ltd had come the redoubtable Mr Hawkins, founder of East Surrey and apparent creator of the Green Line 'brand'.

Compared with the hectic first three years of Green Line's existence, the remaining period up to the outbreak of World War 2 in September 1939 was relatively calm, with little change to the network once the last of the independents had been taken over in early 1934. Unfortunately, Green Line's profitability had been adversely affected by the events of 1933, in particular the joining up of routes to avoid terminating in the capital and the restrictions on picking up passengers. In the 12 months following the October 1933 reorganisation, Green Line lost around one quarter of its passengers and revenue, resulting in surplus vehicles and staff redundancies. Fortunately, Green Line had the protection of the LPTB empire behind it and, despite not being the money-spinner that had been predicted, nevertheless was able to carry on much as usual. The priority was to adjust and consolidate the existing services through increased marketing of the brand-name and more attractive fare structures such as cheap returns and season tickets. A revised route-lettering system was introduced in 1935.

Probably the most significant feature of the second half of the 1930s was the renewal of the coach fleet. As a result of the acquisition of the independents and/or their services, Green Line had inherited a motley assortment of vehicles, composed mainly of Gilfords, Leylands and non-standard Regals, and was now seeking modernisation and standardisation. In 1935, an order was placed for 100 new coaches to replace 87 Gilfords and 12 downgraded Regals.

The first batch of 50 vehicles consisted of AEC Regals designated 9T9 and numbered T403-452. Entering service between June and November 1936, these handsome coaches were unique in having the bonnet and front wings attached to the body, hence the bulbous gaiter across the radiator. An all-metal Weymann body was fitted, complete with 30 comfortable seats, saloon heater and clock. But the 9T9s had some serious short-comings: the 7.7-litre engine was inadequate for coach work. Moreover, the gangways were narrow and maintenance was more difficult. As a result, most of these vehicles were soon downgraded to bus work.

The second batch of 50 coaches consisted of Park Royal-bodied Qs, designated 6Q6 and numbered Q189-238, which entered service from December 1936. With their full fronts and side-mounted engines, these nippy 32-seaters were ahead of their time in terms of appearance. Special features included a raised floor which enabled all the seats to face forward apart from those over the engine, a heater and an air intake in the form of a grille at the front. Although rather claustrophobic to travel in when full, these Q-type coaches proved successful in service.

The same cannot be said for a batch of Qs designated 4Q4 and numbered Q81-105, 186 and 187. These vehicles, with Birmingham Carriage & Wagon Co bodies, were built as buses in 1935 and converted into so-called coaches late in 1936. Some 6Q6 features were added: luggage racks, heaters, air-intake grille, sliding door and roofboard mountings. But the engines were noisy and the seats uncomfortable over long journeys. Consequently, they were normally confined to short routes and not used on cross-London workings. After about a year in service, they were downgraded to buses, and one is left to surmise what the purpose was for this costly, short-lived measure other than, perhaps, to portray the modern image of a full-fronted vehicle as a contrast to the traditional upright-radiator/half-cab types.

The next coaches needing replacement were the remaining acquired vehicles such as the Leyland Tigers and Titans and the original 251 AEC Regals from 1930-1, along with the 27 converted Qs. This objective was achieved by the ordering of 266 traditional-looking AEC Regals (designated 10T10) and 75 Leylands of more radical appearance and engineering. The 10T10s were fine vehicles and the mainstay of Green Line

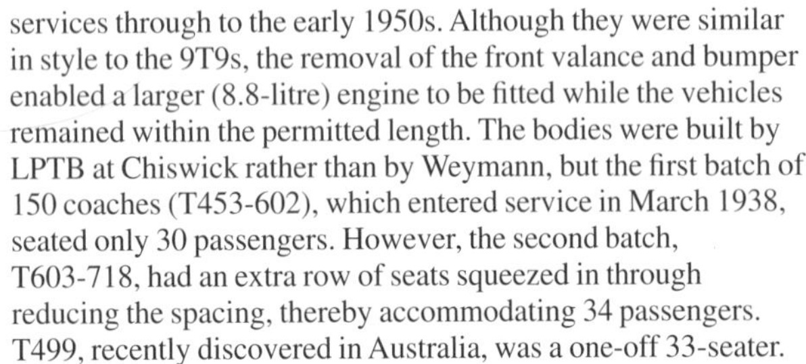

services through to the early 1950s. Although they were similar in style to the 9T9s, the removal of the front valance and bumper enabled a larger (8.8-litre) engine to be fitted while the vehicles remained within the permitted length. The bodies were built by LPTB at Chiswick rather than by Weymann, but the first batch of 150 coaches (T453-602), which entered service in March 1938, seated only 30 passengers. However, the second batch, T603-718, had an extra row of seats squeezed in through reducing the spacing, thereby accommodating 34 passengers. T499, recently discovered in Australia, was a one-off 33-seater.

The final type of prewar Green Line coach was the Leyland FEC (flat-engined coach), numbered in the series TF14-88, plus the prototype (TF1) which dated from 1937. Like the Qs, these vehicles were revolutionary in design and appearance. An 8.6-litre engine was mounted on its side under the floor, and an AEC pre-selective gearbox was fitted. Apart from the prototype, the Green Line TFs carried Chiswick-built 34-seat bodies, and the sloping radiator grille on the nearside provided an excellent view for the lucky two passengers sitting at the front alongside the driver. The first TFs entered service in March 1939, but the onset of the war in September 1939 meant that the last two to be delivered (TFs 14 and 76) started work as ambulances and not as coaches. On 31 August 1939, the Green Line fleet consisted of 266 10T10s, 74 TFs, 34 9T9s, 49 6Q6s, one early T and one 4Q4.

To continue the story, it is necessary to step back a year. War clouds were gathering in 1938 and in June, the Home Office and

The pinnacle of coach design for Green Line services in the immediate prewar period was achieved by two very different classes: the conventional-looking AEC Regal 10T10 and the Leyland Tiger Flat Engined Coach (TF). Here are two examples seen in operation after the war.

◄◄ T524 stands at Epping on 20 May 1951 while working a 718 service to Windsor, the vehicle having served with the US forces in Ashchurch, Gloucestershire from September 1942 to November 1945. Following withdrawal in May 1953, the vehicle, like several of its type, was sold for export. *C. Carter*

◄ TF84, from Hertford garage, like many of the 10T10s, was repainted into bus livery at the end of its Green Line career, and is pictured at Potters Bar. *Geoff Rixon*

LPTB devised a scheme for converting Green Line coaches into ambulances for evacuating patients from central London hospitals and generally helping with casualties if a bombing campaign began. The necessary equipment — stretcher-carriers etc — was stored in the garages where the coaches were based.

On 31 August 1939, the plans were put into action. Green Line coach services were suspended (albeit a few routes continued for another day or so). When vehicles finished their journeys on that date, they were converted overnight, transferred to Central Area garages and were on the streets of London on 1 September 1939 as ambulances. Everyone then waited for the aerial onslaught to begin immediately following the declaration of war on 3 September, but it was a year coming. By October, it was clear that the loss of Green Line coach services was causing real hardship, particularly in the Eastern area. LPTB had obtained permission in 1937 to run double-deckers and decided to take advantage of this. On 1 November, services recommenced with STLs, and in the following month some 9T9s and 10T10s were released, enabling a steady build-up of the network to begin.

In autumn 1940, the Blitz finally arrived and brought chaos to public transport. Green Line abandoned cross-London services; all routes terminated in the capital, and on 4 December a numbering system was introduced to replace the familiar letters. The numbers were chosen at random, using those which were vacant at the time. Yet, despite the restricted coach network, passenger traffic grew, exceeding prewar levels.

In 1942, as the war reached a critical point, the need to conserve fuel and rubber became paramount and, on 29 September, Green Line services were withdrawn for a period which lasted 3½ years. The coach Qs and TFs continued to serve as ambulances, and the 9T9s and 10T10s which had re-entered service were either converted back to ambulances or loaned to the resident US forces. Early Ts from the 1930-1 batches were brought out of store and put to miscellaneous humanitarian uses. But as the war continued, so optimism grew and a team was formed at Reigate, under Arthur Hawkins, to plan the reinstatement of services when hostilities ceased. It was a case of playing a waiting game.

In May 1940, AEC Q-type Q230 was on ambulance duty outside Whittington Hospital (Archway Wing). *John Aldridge collection* ▲

Postwar Revival (1946-1960)

The end of the war in Europe came in May 1945, and the authorities' first priority was to restore bus services to normal. Coach operation would have to wait and, in any case, the process of releasing and refurbishing Green Line vehicles from their wartime uses and obtaining staff would take time. When services did resume, there would be no return to lettered routes; instead, numbers in the 700 series would be used. Theoretically, these would start at Gravesend and continue in a clockwise direction round to Tilbury but, in the event, there were several inconsistencies. At the start, there were 26 routes, numbered from 701 to 727, missing out 719.The latter was earmarked for a Windsor to Luton service which, on introduction, became an express bus route instead. In fact, it was not until July 1956 that route 719 appeared, and this one operated at first from Hemel Hempstead to Victoria.

Green Line recommenced operations on 6 February 1946 with routes 715 and 720, and the remaining services were introduced over the next 5½ months. Many of the new routes mirrored those in operation before the war, albeit on a reduced scale, but there were some changes, in particular, retreating from some of the outer extremities of the network such as Baldock, Edenbridge and Horsham. Evidence that the network had shrunk came from the fact that 100 fewer vehicles were now required. Modifications were also made to the external appearance of the fleet, such as the route blinds becoming black on yellow and the roofboards gold on green.

As regards vehicles, the attractive but underpowered 9T9s were quickly relegated to bus duties, but the Qs remained in favour. These were allocated to routes 724 and 725 operating out of Amersham and High Wycombe, and route 715, based at Hertford and Guildford. The TFs were allocated to routes 712, 713 and 714, working from Luton, St Albans and Dorking garages, as well as route 723 from Grays. All remaining services were in the hands of stalwart 10T10s, with the exception of double-deck routes 721 and 722. For those routes, 10 STLs and 37 wartime austerity Daimlers (all simply buses painted in Green Line livery and devoid of advertisements) were provided by Romford garage. A further five Daimlers were later added to replace the STLs.

Green Line restarted operations with a captive market due to petrol rationing and the scarcity of new cars. In 1947 passenger levels rose by 4% compared with 1938/9, to over 25 million, the introduction of day-return and weekly tickets later in 1946 no doubt helping. In 1948, the LPTB was replaced by the London Transport Executive under the control of the British Transport Commission. That year saw passenger numbers increasing to 26 million, but then a slight drop occurred over the next two years. Routes 721 and 722 found

◄ Two veteran coaches, ex-Bucks Expresses T391 and ex-Green Line T273, are seen in their last few months of service, operating as buses at Kingston in 1949. *Geoff Rixon*

Route 712 from Dorking to Luton was introduced on 29 May 1946. Two TF coaches (TF39 in front) find plenty of passengers at Golders Green.
Albert Dunkley

T267, photographed in Kingston in 1950, was one of the 31 second-series Ts which received Weymann all-metal bodies in 1938 following the decision to withdraw the Reliance chassis to which these bodies had originally been fitted in 1935.
Geoff Rixon

◄ Shown previously on page 19, Kingston's Dodson-bodied T391 (ex-T307) is seen here shortly before its withdrawal in June 1949. Entering service in October 1931 with Bucks Expresses (Watford) Ltd, the vehicle was acquired by Green Line along with that company's Watford to Oxford Circus route on 20 February 1932. *Geoff Rixon*

themselves competing with newly-electrified suburban rail services into Liverpool Street station, and in May 1950 petrol rationing ended. However, in October 1950 LT introduced a new fare structure which enabled Green Line to be more competitively priced with bus and rail travel. From then on, passenger numbers began to grow again, reaching the all-time high of 36 million in 1957, 1959 and 1960.

Another factor which contributed to Green Line's success was the introduction of services to cater for the new towns under development on the fringes of LT's territory: Hatfield, Stevenage, Welwyn Garden City and Harlow. Furthermore, between 1951 and 1956, seven entirely new routes came into operation, the most noteworthy being the 725 southern orbital service, avoiding Central London. Introduced on 1 July 1953, the route ran from Gravesend to Windsor via Croydon and Kingston, and was very successful. Indeed, it is surprising that other orbital routes were not introduced around this time. 1953 was also significant for the large number of extra services laid on for HM The Queen's Coronation in June, which doubtless helped towards the 3 million extra passengers carried that year. However, on a sadder note, the splendid multi-coloured tickets were withdrawn in August.

On the vehicle front, it was proposed that all Green Line services be operated by double-deckers, the requirement being 386 purpose-built coaches of an entirely new design. As a stop-gap, a batch of RTs would be used with platform doors and

This 1948 view of summer seasonal route 726 from Baker Street to Whipsnade Zoo shows D143 arriving at Golders Green. This was one of 37 Duple-bodied wartime austerity Daimlers sent to Romford garage in March 1946 for certain Aldgate routes. *Geoff Rixon collection*

heaters fitted. RT97, one of the experimental pay-as-you-board vehicles, had been tried out in 1946 and ran successfully when used in conventional mode with mobile conductors. As a result, RT97 underwent a complete metamorphosis into a 46-seat luxury coach and emerged as RTC1 in 1949, ready for Green Line duty. Unfortunately, its 'high-tech' specification caused too many problems and it was quickly exiled to a quiet bus route. In the meantime, LT abandoned the idea of a 100% double-deck coach fleet and opted to stay with single-deckers except for the busy Aldgate services, which were in the hands of the somewhat basic Daimlers (for routes 721, 722 and summer-only 726), and TFs (route 723). The Daimlers were replaced in 1950 by standard RTs whose only distinguishing features were Green Line livery, absence of advertisements and a raised bullseye motif on each side, between the decks. The first batch consisted of 36 vehicles (RT3224-3259); a further 49 RTs were added to the Green Line fleet over the next 10 years, but with a gold transfer in place of the raised motif.

Undoubtedly, the most significant event in terms of fleet renewal was the entry into service, initially at Tunbridge Wells (for route 704), of the underfloor-engined AEC Regal IV (RF class) in October 1951. The first 25 members of the class were sightseeing coaches, 27ft 6in long, but this limit, set in January 1932, was extended to 30ft, for single-deckers only, in June

The loss of real Green Line coaches from Romford's Aldgate routes in favour of austerity double-deck buses following the postwar resumption of services was a gain for other routes such as the lengthy 712. TF23 seeks passengers at St Albans.
Ian Allan Library

Looking remarkably compact and cosy (some might say claustrophobic!), Q204 hurries on its way from Hertford to Guildford. It seems extraordinary that such a futuristic design should date back to 1932. There were 232 production single-decker Qs, and the 77 employed on Green Line duties were easily distinguishable externally by the front air-intake grille for the heating system.
Ian Allan Library

The 1936-built 9T9s continued on bus work until 1952, although they were not ideally suited to this work because of their narrow gangways. This view at Bell Common on 20 May 1951 depicts T418 working a Central Area (red) bus route while still carrying its former Green Line coach livery, but with the London Transport fleetname. *C. Carter*

1950. This enabled the 263 Green Line RF coaches to be built to the new length, thereby accommodating 39 passengers. The RFs, with bodywork by Metro-Cammell, were very quiet vehicles and provided an exceptionally smooth ride. However, they were rather heavy and expensive (the RT was 5cwt lighter and cost only £50 more!). Nevertheless, the money was well spent because several members of the class clocked up over 25 years on Green Line service — a record unlikely ever to be beaten.

The arrival of the RFs led to the phasing out of the faithful but archaic-looking 10T10s on Green Line services, although some continued on relief duties after the last RF coaches entered service in July 1952. It was not long, however, before the RFs, and the RTs operating out of Romford and Grays, had the monopoly of all the routes, which remained the case until 1962, with the exception of the prototype 55-seat Routemaster coach, CRL4 (later RMC4), which entered service in October 1957. Out of an eventual LT fleet of 2,760 Routemasters, CRL4 was the least standard of them all, with its combination of Eastern Coach Works body and Leyland running units.

It is worth mentioning that, despite its modern and stylish appearance, the Regal IV type was quickly superseded by a new generation of lighter-weight vehicles. As early as 1953, LT started testing hired single-deckers to determine the extent of fuel economies and whether the vehicles could withstand the rigours of Green Line service. Had LT been sufficiently impressed, some orders would no doubt have been placed because, with the development of new towns and large housing estates, additional Green Line coaches were required. In the end, LT settled for more RFs, and in 1956 35 were converted into coaches, these being plucked from the Central Area, Country Area and Private Hire

The Coronation of HM The Queen in June 1953 created an unprecedented demand for Green Line services into the capital. One of the more unusual vehicles pressed into relief service was this lowbridge double-decker, RLH31, from Guildford garage. *Geoff Rixon*

The last representatives of the famous 'T' class of AEC Regals were the 30 15T13s. These were Country Area buses with bodywork by Mann Egerton of Norwich — the only builder that could offer swift delivery, in this case between March and September 1948. The 15T13s were not normally used as Green Line coaches, but Amersham garage did occasionally utilise its examples for this purpose in the 1950s. The splendid brick garage dating from 1935 has now been demolished and is the site of a supermarket complex, but the original Amersham & District Omnibus & Haulage Co garage on the left, which the LPTB took over in 1933, still survives today. The Amersham company was eventually controlled by the LGOC, and five T-type Green Line coaches operated in Amersham's livery in 1931-3. *John Aldridge collection*

Derek Parsons was busy painting an army lorry at Tampin Camp, Malaya (now Malaysia), in 1954 when he heard the familiar sound of an 8.8-litre AEC engine. Turning round, and almost falling off his ladder in surprise, he saw T708 coming through the gates in full Green Line livery, with route 711 destination blinds and roofboards! The vehicle had been purchased by the WVS and was on its way to Sandicroft Army Leave Centre, Penang, Malaya, to bring a piece of home to the British troops. *Derek Parsons*

This rear view of T791 shows the revised style of Green Line's destination blind introduced in 1955 to replace the type fitted into the front blind box. In addition to the prewar Ford car of advanced design, this scene outside Amersham garage illustrates a typical stylish bus shelter of the mid-1930s. The last members of the 15T13 class were withdrawn in 1962, but sister vehicle T792 was secured for preservation in 1966. T791 was withdrawn in August 1959 and sold to the Ceylon (Sri Lanka) Transport Board.
John Aldridge collection

The first 25 RFs were private-hire coaches, 2ft 6in shorter than the rest of the class, and with glazed panels in the roof. The last 10 were converted to Green Line coaches in 1956; prior to that, the 25 vehicles were sometimes employed on relief duties and in 1955 were used as temporary replacements for RF coaches undergoing cyclical overhaul. RF20, standing outside Northfleet garage in June 1955, displays what was probably the dullest livery ever worn on Green Line service: unrelieved Lincoln green with red lettering, which is why the vehicle seems to be anonymous. The previous livery, with light grey above waist level and red lining, was far more striking. Following the arrival of the first production batch of Routemaster coaches in summer 1962, the 10 short RFs were withdrawn and sold, making these the first members of the class to become redundant.
Ron Stevens

RF211 stands at the former Autocar coach station at Tunbridge Wells on 27 October 1953.
Ron Stevens

◄ Normal bus RTs were frequent performers on Green Line relief duties, but the use of a roofbox RT with route number displayed in the box was less common. RT989 was photographed in Dartford on a Coronation service. Of the 85 Green Line-liveried RTs, 62 were converted to bus livery in 1965, and the final 23 were regraded as buses in November 1969. *Ron Stevens*

fleets. Some were put immediately into use for two services introduced in 1956: route 719 (Hemel Hempstead-Victoria via Garston) and route 715A (Hertford-Marble Arch via Edmonton). Most of the remainder were used to strengthen existing services due to increasing patronage.

When 1960 arrived, Green Line was still on a roll. Peak-hour vehicle requirements had risen by 28% over the last decade, and continued growth was still expected. Orders were placed for the next generation of double-deckers, this time purpose-built Routemaster coaches. As a stop-gap, a further 28 RTs were fitted with heaters and painted in Green Line livery, replacing ordinary bus RTs which had been drafted in as additional relief vehicles. Consideration was also given to brightening up the rather sombre livery; 16 RFs and CRL4 were repainted into pale green, although this experiment was later abandoned. 1960 produced passenger numbers equalling 1959's — a very creditable performance, but a plateau had now been reached. From now on, Green Line would be on the slide.

▸ Unlike other prototypes, CRL4 (later RMC4) was a highly-successful guinea-pig. This handsome Leyland vehicle, carrying a unique Eastern Coach Works body seating 57 passengers (instead of the normal 64), started work in October 1957 at Romford garage on RT-operated route 721. This view shows CRL4 immediately on entry into service, with plenty of passengers, but no driver. On 30 December 1957, CRL4 went to High Wycombe garage for trials on route 711. *John Aldridge collection*

Decline and Fall (1961-1976)

By the close of 1961, it had become apparent that the previous year had marked a turning point in Green Line's fortunes. Passenger journeys in 1961 were 5.2% below 1960's level, and this was attributed to several factors: increased competition from the railways through modernisation and cheap return fares, fewer shopping trips due to the development of better local shops, and the increasing volume of road traffic upsetting schedules. Yet vehicle requirements remained high: 219 RFs and 57 RTs in 1962. However, to maintain profitability, service cuts became the order of the day, and this was particularly evident when the first production Routemaster coaches (RMCs) started work on 27 August 1962. These 57-seaters, with their deep-cushioned seats, fluorescent lighting, luggage racks and platform doors, created new standards and were expected to attract extra passengers. Unfortunately, in many cases, their introduction brought reductions in service frequency which, not surprisingly, had a negative effect on the public, even though it was sensible economically . The arrival of the 68 production RMCs started the erosion of the RF's 10 year domination, 75 being displaced.

As a result of the decline in patronage, Green Line had to find ways of arresting this trend. One idea was to shorten journey times by reducing stops. In August 1963, the first Express service was introduced, on the Windsor to London section of the 705 route to Sevenoaks. This was followed in April 1964 by the re-routing of the 726 service, bringing Green Line for the first time on to a motorway (the M1). Later that year, in November, route 709 became an Express service between Amersham and Oxford Circus and, at the same time a new Express route, the 727, again using the M1, was introduced between Tring and Victoria. Interestingly, the route included Piccadilly Circus and Trafalgar Square, making this the first Green Line service to travel through Central London since the 1933 restrictions. The result of these initiatives, combined with minor changes to other services, brought about a slight increase in Green Line mileage in 1964, but, after that, the network started to shrink. Indeed, none of the new ventures proved successful in the long run, and all operated for only a short time. Part of the problem was attributed to the Country RF's modest maximum speed of 53mph, coupled with motorway roadworks and worsening traffic congestion. Another disastrous venture had been the extension of route 722, which was an attempt to join Essex and Kent via the new Dartford Tunnel.

In 1965, the lengthened Routemaster coaches (RCLs) were introduced, mainly replacing the RTs. There were 43 such vehicles, carrying 65 passengers (nine more than the RTs), but sadly the coaches came too late. The routes they served no longer needed the increased seating capacity and, in any case, LT now had other ideas for making the Green Line network more cost-effective: one-person operation (OPO). Ironically, this would give a life-extension to the RF fleet, which could be easily converted but would cause the early demotion of the Routemaster coaches to bus work. LT believed that Green Line's future would be safe in the hands of a modern single-deck coach fleet. As a start, 14 new AEC Reliance coaches (designated RC) were purchased, and entered service on 28 November 1965 on route 705. These vehicles carried 49-seat Willowbrook bodies and, taking advantage of the new permitted maximum dimensions, were 36ft long and 8ft 2½in wide. They were well appointed, with high-backed seats and footrests, large panoramic windows and adjustable ventilation for each passenger, and carried a new silver-grey livery with green relief band.

Whilst the RCs certainly looked impressive, they were nevertheless an experimental type, and it was clear that Green Line would have to rely on RFs for a few more years. The decision was therefore taken to modernise the interior and exterior of these vehicles, starting with RF136. The main changes were fluorescent lighting, twin headlamps, one-piece windscreen, and external aluminium strips which created a broad relief band of pale green to contrast with the retained Lincoln green colour for the remainder of the bodywork. RF136 re-entered service in March 1966 and its 'makeover' was deemed a great success. Consequently, another 174 RFs were similarly treated, representing current RF requirements, and these returned to service between August 1966 and September 1967. Whether it was wise to refurbish 15-year-old vehicles, each of which had travelled around one million miles, is debatable. However, no-one could dispute the RF's reliability and stamina, which was more than could be said for the RCs. These had to be replaced on route 705 by RCLs after only two years and were then withdrawn temporarily for re-evaluation.

As regards the Green Line network itself, there was some good news to report: the launching of two successful express routes, neither of which touched Central London. On 10 July 1966, the second orbital route commenced operation, some 13 years after the pioneer 725 service. This new route (724) ran from Romford to High Wycombe, a distance of 70 miles, and was notable for being the first OPO Green Line route. The other new route, which started on 13 May 1967, was the 727, using the number from the withdrawn Tring to Victoria service. The new 727 was also an OPO orbital route, and ran from Luton to Gatwick Airport via Heathrow Airport. This marathon journey of 74 miles, with only 25 stops, was scheduled to take 3½ hours, running at an average speed of 21mph, and making this the longest and fastest Green Line route. Since the 727 served two airports (Luton Airport had to wait because this was outside LT's operating area), the RFs were fitted with extra luggage space, reducing seating capacity from 39 to 35 passengers. An innovative concept was a through booking facility for rail travellers to Heathrow (and later Gatwick) Airport from Luton and Watford Junction stations.

Experience with routes 724 and 727 convinced LT that economies necessary to sustain the viability of the Green Line operation could be achieved through extending OPO to all single-deck services. This was carried out in two tranches, on 23 November 1968 and 15 February 1969. However, this measure addressed only the cost-saving issue. There was still a major problem over declining patronage. Already, 24 of the modernised RFs had become redundant after only two years, and were downgraded to buses. By the end of the decade, passenger numbers had fallen by 42% since 1960; indeed, taking into account that passengers were now using Green Line routes over shorter distances, the volume of lost business over the decade was nearer 50%. This was not an attractive legacy to pass down to London Country Bus Services (LCBS), the new National Bus Company subsidiary which took over LT's Country Bus & Coach Department on 1 January 1970, following the transfer of responsibility for Central Area services to the Greater London Council. This was the biggest change to affect Green Line since the company was absorbed by the LPTB in 1933.

LCBS inherited a coach operation which was making considerable losses and whose fleet requirement of 130 single-deckers and 80 double-deckers was made up of largely outdated vehicles. Apart from the RCs, the fleet belonged to existing LT classes, and LT had first call on spare parts and maintenance facilities; it was not until 1976 that LCBS had its own overhaul works. The familiar pattern of operations continued: reductions in frequencies, increases in fares and curtailments of underused services. However, one benefit arising from the split with LT was that Green Line routes could now be extended beyond former boundaries. Consequently, in 1971, route 727 entered United Counties' territory to reach Luton Airport, and the 704 and 705 penetrated Alder Valley's area to serve Windsor Safari Park (now Legoland).

LCBS was anxious to achieve 100% OPO on Green Line services as quickly as possible, which meant the replacement of the coach Routemasters. Their successors were 90 AEC Reliance coaches (designated RP), fitted with 45-seat Park Royal bodies, which entered service from December 1971. The RMCs and RCLs were then demoted to bus work, apart from four (later three) RCLs rostered until May 1976 at Godstone garage for peak-hour operation on route 709. The RPs looked formidable in their livery of Lincoln green and pale green wide relief band, but never carried the famous wooden roof boards which had just been phased out. However, the RPs did not prove very reliable, mainly due to a lack of the necessary garage skills and inadequate flows of spares. Consequently, many were downgraded to bus work after a mere seven years of service, and some were even withdrawn then, due to a recertification 'bulge' affecting various classes of buses and coaches which had entered service seven years earlier.

The next priority was to replace the RFs, which were now over 20 years old. With delays in delivery times for new vehicles, LCBS began the replacement programme by obtaining 21 new AEC Swifts (the SMA class) which had been originally ordered by South Wales Transport. Their 45-seat Alexander bodies provided wonderful viewing facilities for passengers because of their ramped floor and large windows, but, once again, there were shortcomings in the mechanical department — in this case, unreliability and inadequate engine power. The SMAs entered service in March 1972 and replaced RFs on the 725 southern orbital route, being generally confined to this service and the linked 726 route. These coaches introduced a lighter-green livery to Green Line services, and were also the last class to be fitted with rear destination blinds; unusually, these were positioned below window level. However, the SMA class lasted in service for barely seven years.

An interesting route revision which occurred in 1972 was the withdrawal of the 724 Express service between High Wycombe and Rickmansworth, and its extension to Heathrow Airport and

GREEN LINE

COACH SERVICES To OXFORD CIRCUS and CHARING CROSS

BOOK ON THE COACH OR AT ANY BOOKING AGENT.

CHILDREN'S FARES.—Children under 14 years of age half-price (except where otherwise stated). All children, except infants in arms, must be paid for.

CONDITIONS.—The Company will make every effort to maintain the scheduled service, but cannot accept any responsibility for inconvenience, loss, damage, or breakdown, or anything arising from unavoidable causes. **Small hand luggage carried free at owner's risk.**

Operated by

EAST SURREY TRACTION CO., LTD., REIGATE
'PHONE: REIGATE 593.

AUTOCAR SERVICES, LTD., TUNBRIDGE WELLS
'PHONE: TUN. WELLS 1267.

12/11/30

ISSUED FREE

Bell Street
Reigate
Surrey
REIGATE 1200

GREEN LINE Coaches can be hired for

RACE MEETINGS, THEATRE AND CONCERT PARTIES, FIRMS' OUTINGS, ETC.

No Job too small. No Job too large.

For suggestions and rates apply

HIRE DEPARTMENT,

55, Broadway, S.W. 1. Telephone: Victoria 6800.

◂ The fronts of three early Green Line guides (reduced in size) are depicted here. The earliest dates from 12 November 1930 and gives the operators of Green Line coach services as East Surrey Traction Co Ltd of Reigate and Autocar Services Ltd of Tunbridge Wells. Details of 10 services are provided, all at this stage unlettered and unnumbered: these are London (Oxford Circus) to Sevenoaks, Tunbridge Wells, East Grinstead (Crown), Godstone Green, Oxted (Hoskins Arms), Great Bookham (Victoria), Dorking (Falkland Arms), Reigate (Red Cross), Crawley (George); also London (Charing Cross) to Guildford (Horse and Groom). By the time the February 1931 guide was published, there were 34 routes separately listed, 16 operating out of the new Poland Street Coach Station. By 1935, Issue 1, there were 33 differently-lettered services. *Author's collection*

◂ Early marketing effort, taken from the February 1931 *Coach Service Guide*. *Author's collection*

▲ This scene at Reigate garage on 27 August 1961 shows RF271 wearing the experimental pale green livery applied to 16 RFs and CRL4 in 1960. The application of black to the front wheelnut ring and around the outer edge of the rear wheel discs is an interesting detail. The pale green livery was not adopted, although the lighter green relief was chosen to accompany the standard Lincoln green which remained the main colour for Green Line coaches. *Gerald Mead*

◄ RF150 heads south along Petersham Road, Richmond, towards the junction with Star & Garter Hill in June 1964. The coach is well filled, although it is unlikely that any passengers originate from Luton, where the route commenced. *Mike Harries*

0 7298

LONDON TRANSPORT
FT COACHES C.S.11

8	Dunstable The Square	Stock[illegible] Station	37
9	Dustable Emp Rubbr Wrks	Vauxhall Station	36
10	H[illegible] & Jockey Watling St	London Marble Arch Victoria or Hyde Park Cr	35
11	Markyate White Hrt		
12	F[illegible] Wash The Chequrs	Baker Street Station	34
13	Redbourn Aysgarth R	Kings Cross & St Pncrs Stn	33
14	Redbourn The Elms	Camden Rd York Way	32
15	Punch Bowl Redbourn R	Archway Station	31
16	S[illegible] Bridge	Highgate Station	30
17	St Albans Mayles Cnr London Rd	East Finchley Bald Faced Stag	29
10	Luton Park Square	North Fnchly Tally Ho	28
11	L[illegible] Fields	Whetstone [illegible] Inn	27
12	K[illegible] Grn The Harrow	Barnet Church	26
13	Harpenden The George	Green Dragon [illegible] Mimms	25
14	Harpenden C WestCom W	South Mimms White Hart	24
15	C[illegible] Lodge	Waggn & Hor S. Mimms	23
16	B[illegible]wood [illegible] Btn	Finchley Rd [illegible] Station	33
17	St. Albans ChqerSt LR	Golders Grn Station	32
18	London Rd Mile House	Hendon Cen Station	31
19	London Colny Kings Rd	Page Street Watford W	30
20	The Bell LondnColny	Mill Hill Broadway	29
21	Bell Lane Napsbury L	Watford Way Apex Cnr	28
22	Shenley Black Lion	Barnet B-P Stirling Cnr	27
23	Radlett Red Lion	Elstree Station	26
24	Butterfly Lane	Allum Lane Corner	25

Bell Punch Company, Ltd., London.

Staines via the Cargo Tunnel. A few years earlier, while serving on the BAA Passenger Transport Panel, I had suggested running a bus route through this tunnel, secretly hoping that green RTs would fraternise with red ones in the Central Terminal Area. Unfortunately, LT's response was that this would not be possible because the tunnel was in a Customs Controlled area (ie 'airside') which, for security reasons, precluded the use of open-platform vehicles.

The updating of the Green Line fleet continued with the ordering of Leyland Nationals to replace the remaining RFs. However, the choice of type was to cause considerable harm to the network's image. Leyland Vehicles initially declined to produce an upgraded coach version, and so the first vehicles were of bus specification, with plastic-covered seats and unacceptable noise levels for longer-distance travel. The first batch numbered 47 units (LNC24-70), which were painted in the new National Bus Company (NBC) livery of leaf green and white. They entered service from February 1973, initially replacing not RFs but RPs only one year old, which were moved to other Green Line duties. The LNCs were followed by 40 shorter Leyland Nationals in the SNC series (being 1m shorter than the LNCs). The plastic seats were covered in moquette, which gave a better appearance until the moquette wore through, but in all other respects, these vehicles were just buses. Finally, 87 proper Leyland National coaches arrived, with 39 coach-type seats, plus overhead luggage racks and an improved level of

Following the failure of the RT coach experiment, and needing a suitable replacement for the wartime austerity Daimlers, LT allocated a batch of 36 Weymann-bodied RTs to Green Line use. This first batch (RT3224–3259), despite being just ordinary RTs, looked special because of the absence of external advertising and the addition of a raised 'Green Line' motif between the decks, effectively preventing any attempt to apply a side poster. Application of the 'Green Line' fleetname added the finishing touch to the RT coach illusion. RT3224 stands at Corbets Tey, the Upminster terminus of route 722, on 28 March 1965. *Gerald Mead* ▸

▸▸ Brand-new '**R**outemaster **C**oach **L**ong' RCL2235 looks superb as it picks up passengers in Chadwell Heath in June 1965. Unfortunately, the drive towards complete OPO on Green Line services meant demotion to bus work for all but four of the 43-strong class by the early 1970s. *Maurice Bateman*

overall comfort. However, not even the Leyland National coaches were able to stop the rot; they still failed to convey the image of a comfortable express-coach service.

These were increasingly difficult times for Green Line in many other respects, with various problems occurring simultaneously: high inflation, a non-standard fleet, inadequate overhaul facilities, a nationwide lack of vehicle spare parts, staff shortages, increasing traffic congestion and accelerating losses, with inevitable service cuts. The pride and prestige of the Green Line operation was no longer there. By 1976, almost any vehicle might be turned out for Green Line duty, however battered or scruffy, with paper labels stuck over the blinds. Crew operation was meant to have ceased on 15 May 1976 when route 709 was converted from RCL to SNC operation, yet until early 1977 Tring was employing an RT on Green Line work and a few RMCs and RMLs were put to such use through to 1979. In the mid-1970s there were also several 25-year-old RFs still on Green Line duty, including unmodernised ones, and stranger vehicles such as Bristol LHSs (BNs) and hired buses; even XF-class Daimler Fleetlines could turn up. The variety kept enthusiasts happy but did nothing to endear the coach services to the travelling public. Green Line was becoming an embarrassment, and something had to be done; closure of the network or a relaunch with a new image were the only options.

GREEN LINE
721
Gallows Corner Romford
Goodmayes Ilford
Stratford Bow
BRENTWOOD
LONDON HOSPITAL ANNEXE
LONDON TRANSPORT
GREEN LINE
RCL 2235
RE 9
CUV 235 C
BUTLER
FISH
MERCHANT

Famous for being the last RF to run in normal service in London, RF202 stands at Victoria on 28 May 1966. The vehicle acquired this fleetnumber on overhaul in January 1964 and kept it for the rest of its working life. Within four months of this photograph being taken, RF202 became one of the 175 modernised RFs.
Gerald Mead

◄ A radical but short-lived livery change occurred when the 14 RC-class AEC Reliance coaches entered service in November 1965. These were powerful and comfortable vehicles, but were beset with unreliability problems. This view shows RC12 at Hyde Park Corner in October 1967. *Vernon Murphy*

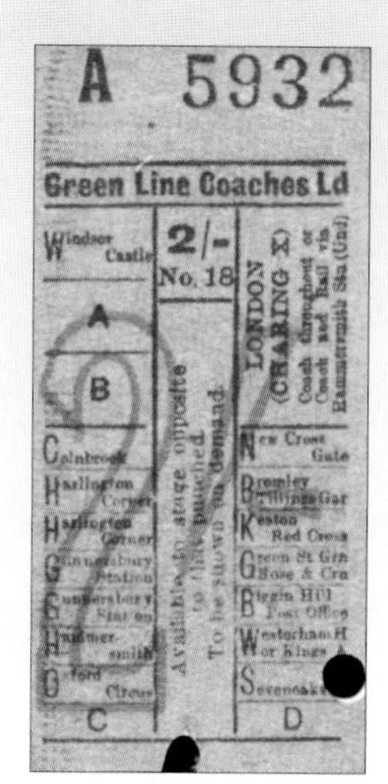

Numerically the earliest Green Line RT was RT600, seen here at Victoria on 26 May 1967. This was one of a batch of 16 RTs painted into Green Line livery in 1960 for relief duties. The Green Line 'bullseye' between the decks was merely a transfer and not a raised motif, the latter feature being confined to the first 36 vehicles. *John Aldridge*

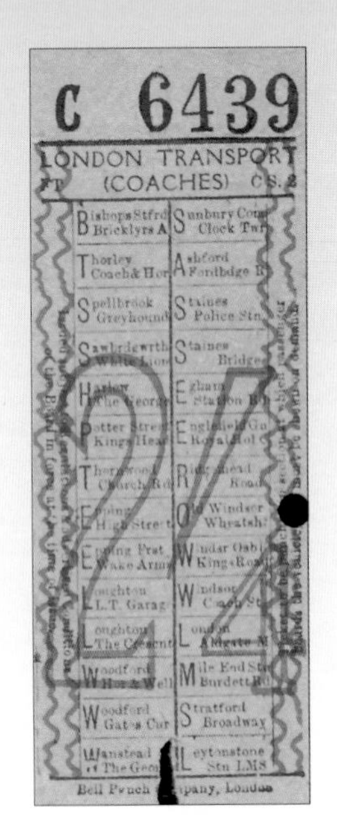

◄ When the 68 production normal-length Routemaster coaches entered service in 1962 they carried the traditional Green Line fleetname with the words 'London Transport' added, and a raised 'bullseye' between the decks. Following their first overhaul, the appearance of the RMCs was brought into line with the later RCLs with the applications of the plain Green Line fleetname and a transfer between the decks instead of the raised motif. RMC1460, with missing radiator triangle, turns out of Guildford High Street towards the Horse and Groom public house in June 1969.
Dave Brown

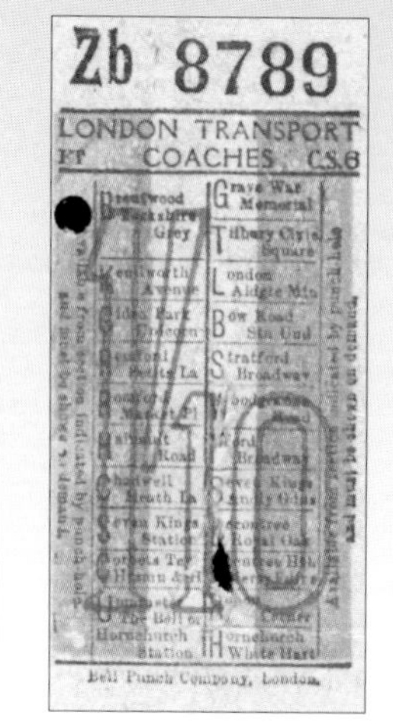
Zb 8789
LONDON TRANSPORT
LT COACHES C.S.6
Bell Punch Company, London

▲ Following the discontinuation of the silver-grey livery, the RC class adopted the modernised RF style of livery. RC14 was photographed climbing up Bell Street, Reigate, in June 1969. The former East Surrey offices on the corner of Lesbourne Road are visible on the left, together with part of the original bus garage. *Mike Harries*

▲ The London Country era has now dawned and the dark LT Lincoln green has given way to a lighter shade. The short-lived 'flying Polo' has also arrived in place of the LT roundel. RC8 waits at the well-established Green Line terminus at Aldgate in early 1973. *Steve Fennell*

GREEN LINE
716 KINGSTON
GREEN LINE
SV 50
JPA 135K
10

◄ It's back to Lincoln green for this view of RP35 at Stevenage in 1973. Unlike the RC coaches, which were essentially an experimental type, the 90 AEC Reliances classified RP were the first coaches to be purchased by London Country and were introduced primarily to replace the Routemaster coaches. Although seating 20 fewer passengers than the RCLs, the RPs brought economies through being OPO vehicles. *Steve Fennell*

▲ As early as 1968, after less than two years of running as modernised coaches, 24 of the 175 Green Line RFs were declared surplus to requirements as a result of service cuts. The vehicles in question were downgraded to buses and were readily distinguishable because the pale green relief band was repainted yellow. In the first half of the 1970s, London Country was reduced to employing any operational RF, regardless of status, to cover for breakdowns which plagued the more modern coaches. Demoted coach RF127 waits to take a 711 service out of the Reigate terminus situated in front of the garage. The date is 22 August 1974. *Michael Furnell*

Displaying the lighter shade of green is SMA8, seen here at Windsor. This vehicle belonged to a class of 21 AEC Swifts ordered by South Wales Transport and diverted to London Country. Although attractive coaches, they were slightly underpowered for Green Line work compared with the RC and RP classes.
Mike Pope

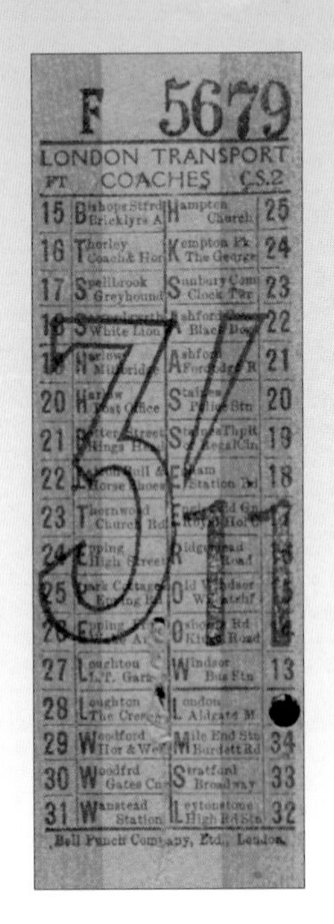

▲ The conversion of Routemaster-operated routes to OPO in 1972 left only one scheduled crew-operated service — the peak-hour and Sunday 709 from Godstone to Baker Street. Four RCLs were originally allocated to Godstone for this purpose; here, on 7 April 1975, RCL2250 is heading home down the A22. The route was converted to OPO on 15 May 1976. *Michael Furnell*

▲ Route 710 from Gravesend to Ascot was withdrawn from 3 October 1975. Epitomising the desperate vehicle situation around this period is the use of unmodernised RF42, seen in Park View Road, Welling, on 26 May (Spring Bank Holiday) 1975, on this normally SNC-operated service. Evidence of the earlier fitting of roofboard support brackets is clearly visible. *Michael Furnell*

◂ Proof that just about any vehicle which was capable of moving could find itself on a Green Line service in the mid-1970s is provided at Purley on 26 July 1975. Daimler Fleetline XF5, complete with red-oxide paint on the roof and chalked route-number, pretends to be a coach. *John Aldridge*

◂ The nadir of Green Line operation was regarded by many as the use of multi-coloured Reliance RP46, which received this garish livery in January 1973 and retained it until August 1976. RP7 and RP87 also gained all-over advertising, for Champion Spark Plugs and Airfix models respectively, but these were visually less stressful. With no hint of green, apart from some garnish on a plate, RP46 waits at Victoria. *Steve Fennell*

▲ Route 720 from Bishop's Stortford (later, Stansted Airport) to Aldgate via Harlow ran for the last time on 1 April 1977. RP39 is seen near the Wakes Arms, Epping Forest, during the final week of service.
Michael Furnell

Renaissance (1977-1987)

With the introduction of local authority subsidies for less remunerative sections of routes and Government grants of 50% for qualifying new vehicles, LCBS took the bold decision to save the coach network and revitalise it. Investment would be made in luxury coaches, new markets would be found and wider publicity opportunities sought. Constraints on capital expenditure were overcome by leasing 150 Duple- and Plaxton-bodied AEC Reliance coaches (the RB and RS classes). These vehicles, hired from a dealer (Kirkby Central), were delivered between 1977 and 1980 on five-year leases. Initial problems over braking were resolved, and these vehicles became very reliable; they also brought unprecedented luxury to Green Line services, and were ideal for the Motorway Express services. The arrival of the RBs and RSs heralded the removal of RPs, SMAs and Leyland Nationals from front-line coach service.

The renaissance continued with the finding of new markets, eg shopping services, and seasonal tourist services providing combined travel and admission fees to places of interest. But the biggest development involved the expansion of the airport services. The pioneer route had been the 727, followed by the re-routing of the 724. In 1977, two new services to Luton Airport (routes 707 and 717) were introduced in January, and from May a variation of the 725 orbital service began, from Gravesend to Windsor but via Heathrow (route 726). Also in May 1977, motivated by the forthcoming Silver Jubilee of HM The Queen, the still-extant non-stop 700 service from London to Windsor was introduced. Then, in May 1978, a new Victoria to Windsor service via Heathrow (route 701) began, followed, in April 1979, by the worldwide-marketed Jetlink 747 route running non-stop between Heathrow and Gatwick airports, which, from 1983, would operate round the clock, 364 days a year. Building on the success of this service, route 757 (Luton Airport to Victoria) was introduced in November 1980, and in May 1981 route 777, linking Victoria and Gatwick, came into operation, worked

▲ The last RF to carry Green Line livery and to operate as a coach in normal service was RF202, pictured here at Hampton Court on 23 April 1978. At this time, unmodernised RF221 was also still in use. RF202 was withdrawn in July 1979 and re-emerged a year later in its 1966 Green Line livery for special duties. Finally withdrawn in July 1989 and robbed of its original registration number (which was transferred to a Leyland Tiger), RF202 now enjoys an active life in preservation in Cornwall. *Geoff Rixon*

▲ London Country put considerable effort into celebrating the Golden Jubilee of Green Line services, and painted several coaches in a special gold livery. One such vehicle was DV1, which was photographed in August 1980 while working the short-lived 734 north/south orbital service to Hertford via Brent Cross, when this shopping facility seemed to be the centre of the universe. DV1 was one of a pair of Duple-bodied Volvos which, together with two Leyland Leopards, were trialled as possible successors to the discontinued AEC Reliance. This view at Ealing Broadway shows, in the background on the right, the former municipal offices dating from 1874 in the Mall. *Geoff Rixon*

▶ In the early 1980s, following its withdrawal from normal service, RMC4 (ex-CRL4) was used on various special Green Line duties — in this case, commemorating the retirement of the last conductress at Garston garage. The vehicle is seen here at Marble Arch, turning into Edgware Road on 20 June 1981. This splendid livery still graces the streets of London regularly, carried by RMC1461 on Stagecoach East London route 15. As for RMC4, this historic vehicle passed into the hands of ARRIVA and has recently been sold into private preservation. *Geoff Rixon*

719
GREEN LINE
RELIEF
HEMEL HEMPSTEAD
GREEN LINE
ROUTEMASTER COACH
ROUTEMASTER COACH
93
GREEN LINE
LONDON TRANSPORT
RMC 4
SLT 59

After the introduction of the first jointly-operated service in 1980, which took Green Line coaches to Oxford, it was not surprising that this should be followed up, in 1981, by a joint service to Cambridge. This photograph, taken in September 1981 at Turnpike Lane, depicts RB81 on Green Line/Eastern Counties route 798. *Geoff Rixon*

A 3459
LONDON TRANSPORT
FT COACHES C.S.B
Bell Punch Company, Ltd, London.

jointly with Southdown. Special liveries and 'Flightline' branding were used for this service and the subsequent 767 route from Victoria to Heathrow, another non-stop joint operation, this time in conjunction with Alder Valley, which started in January 1982. Flightline branding was also extended to route 757.

While new markets were being explored, old routes were being abandoned or radically altered. 27 October 1979 marked the end of cross-London working, with the last two services, routes 715 and 719, now terminating in Central London. A few months earlier, another landmark passed with the withdrawal of LCBS's last RF (202), which was a frequent performer on route 725 right to the end, complete with Green Line fleetnames.

In addition to the new airport routes, Green Line started to develop longer-distance commuter and tourist services, particularly following the deregulation in 1980 of coach services exceeding 30 miles. This enabled Green Line to reach popular attractions such as Oxford, Cambridge and Brighton. Also, by assisting the National Express network, Green Line coaches could be seen at various destinations far removed from London. The first 'over the border' routes were the 290, operated jointly with City of Oxford Motor Services, which began in June 1980, and numbers 797 and 798, which were jointly run with Eastern Counties and took Green Line to Cambridge. The Sealine 773 service brought Green Line to Brighton and Hove from 1982 while, in the same year, a joint working with United Counties created route 760 from Heathrow to Northampton. This number had become available due to a rare example of an unsuccessful new service — commuter route 760, which ran between Croydon and Crawley and lasted only six months in 1981.

During all this expansion there was a recession taking place but, if anything, this was helpful to Green Line because it meant greater unemployment, allowing LCBS to recruit more staff to enable the Green Line network to grow. Opportunities also arose for more commuter services, due particularly to problems in the rail industry — principally deteriorating industrial relations and rising fares. Green Line was able to lure passengers from the railways with the offer of cheap season tickets.

On the fleet front, the early 1980s saw the phased departure of the hired Reliance coaches which had contributed so significantly to Green Line's revival. In their place came a variety of new vehicles, mainly Leyland Tigers with, again, Plaxton or Duple bodies. From March 1984, double-deck working (but on OPO basis) was reintroduced following the arrival of 15 Leyland Olympians with Eastern Coach Works bodies and coach seating.

▲ Route 789, which was meant to be operated by RB coaches from Amersham garage, got off to an ominous start on 16 January 1982 with the rostering of Leyland National SNB125 (previously SNC125) for the journey from Chesham, where this view was taken, to Victoria. The route was short-lived, being withdrawn on 2 October 1982. *Geoff Rixon*

◄ London Country acquired 10 1972-vintage AEC Reliances from Barton Transport in 1977. Their Plaxton Panorama Elite Express bodies carried 66 passengers in rows of 3+2 seating, making them ideal for school duty but less satisfactory for prestigious express-coach work. Consequently, they were classified as buses, despite their external appearance. This view at Surbiton in March 1982 depicts RN2 operating a 714 Green Line service to Capel. The class was taken out of service in 1988-9, so they lasted quite well, given their age and the fact that they were bought second-hand, their longevity reflecting their usefulness on contract work. *Geoff Rixon*

▲ Green Line meets Eastern National at Walthamstow on 13 March 1982. RB127 is working a 702 service to Harlow and Bishop's Stortford which was introduced on 2 April 1977. Until 6 July 1973, this route number was used for a Sunningdale service, running originally from Gravesend. However, the northbound 702 was not long-lived, becoming route 502 on 12 May 1984. One week later, the 702 was going west again, running from Victoria to Windsor Safari Park in place of route 701. *Michael Furnell*

◂ Former Leyland National coach SNB127 (ex-SNC127) finds Green Line work on 15 April 1982 at Bexleyheath clock tower. Daimler Fleetline DMS2005 waits behind. Route 755, which started from Crawley, was withdrawn between West Croydon and Gravesend one month later. *Michael Furnell*

The age of unusual Green Line relief workings was not yet over in the early 1980s, as illustrated here at Cobham on 29 June 1982. The all-over advertising livery of this Park Royal-bodied Leyland Atlantean, built in 1972, looks superb in this shot taken at 8pm. *Geoff Rixon*

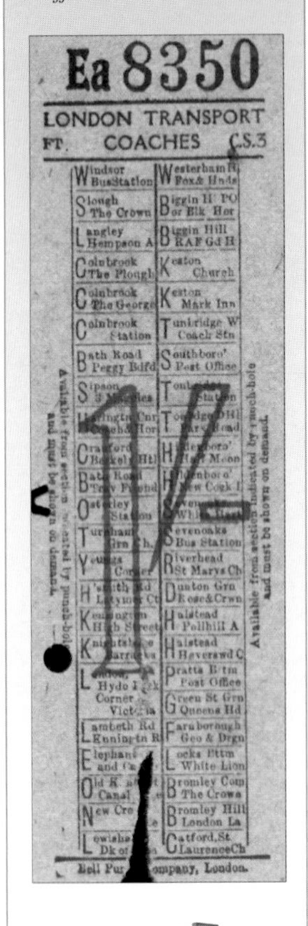

▲ With its Green Line fleetname virtually obliterated from the roof, RP29 has a full load on board as it passes Hyde Park Corner on its way to Farnham on 17 July 1982. The remaining RPs were due for withdrawal that year, and indeed half of the class of 90 had already expired before that. However, the last survivors reached 1984, including RP29 which made the final trip to the scrapyard after 13 years of active service. *Geoff Rixon*

▲ The next generation of Green Line coaches, which overlapped with the phased return of the leased AEC Reliances, was a fleet of 42 Leyland Tigers with Eastern Coach Works bodies, delivered in 1982. TL10 from Windsor garage approaches Hyde Park Corner from Knightsbridge in September 1982. *Geoff Rixon*

▲ Following the TL class came the TDs in 1983 — the first coaches to carry the new, striped Green Line livery. The TDs were Leyland Tigers with Duple Dominant IV bodies and numbered 45. Ten of the class were painted in the Jetlink 747 version of the new livery, including TD32 which was photographed at Hampton Court on 20 May 1983. With their 46 reclining seats, these were, by then, the most comfortable coaches to be used on Green Line services.
Geoff Rixon

▲ London Country's first vehicles bought specifically for private-hire work were five AEC Reliance coaches with Plaxton Panorama Elite bodywork. These entered service in 1974 and were numbered P1-P5. Later painted into Green Line colours as a result of NBC adopting a more liberal attitude to liveries, P1 was photographed at the Scilly Isles roundabout near Hinchley Wood in June 1983. Sister vehicle P3 was acquired by Cobham Bus Museum in 1995 for use on driver training. *Geoff Rixon*

The 747 Jetlink non-stop Heathrow-Gatwick service started on 28 April 1979. This prestigious route used the latest vehicles and had its own special branding. This view of BTL9 at Heathrow on 5 March 1985 was taken shortly after the service was restocked with eight Berkhof-bodied Leyland Tigers, from an eventual class of 53 vehicles. Note the dot-matrix destination display. *Geoff Rixon* ▶

747 GATWICK
Gatwick Heathrow
Jetlink 747
GREEN LINE
GREEN LINE
BTL9
B109 KPF

▲ This scene at Eccleston Square, Victoria, in June 1986 depicts brand-new TDL58, a Leyland Tiger with Duple 320 bodywork. This vehicle belonged to a batch of 20 delivered in 1986 whose fleet numbers were tagged on to the TD class, although they were of totally different appearance. The TDLs were the last coaches ordered by London Country before its break-up into separate companies in readiness for privatisation. Behind TDL58 stands TP23, a Leyland Tiger of more traditional style dating from 1983 and carrying Plaxton Paramount 3200 bodywork. *Geoff Rixon*

A return to second-hand vehicles occurred in 1988/9 when London Country South West (renamed London & Country in April 1989) bought 1983-built Leyland Tigers with Duple Laser bodywork from Shamrock & Rambler, classifying them DLT. On 28 April 1990, DLT6 crosses Hampton Court Bridge on a 715 working to Guildford. *Geoff Rixon*

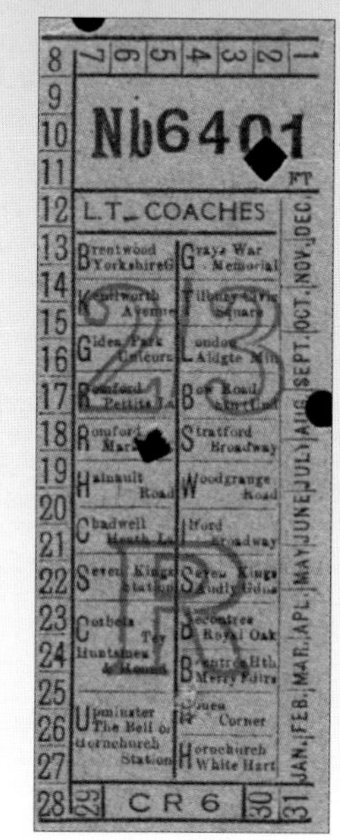

Hiatus and Recovery (1988-2000)

By the mid-1980s, Green Line was flourishing once more, with a fleet of over 300 vehicles, making it the largest coach operator in Britain. Indeed, London Country's fortunes in terms of bus operations were also on an upward trend, largely due to success in winning some lucrative LT tendered services. All was well, until certain external factors intervened. The Government of the day was committed to privatising state-owned entities, and the National Bus Company was regarded as ripe for this treatment. However, when it came to preparing the various NBC subsidiaries for privatisation, London Country (which, of course, included Green Line coaches) was considered to be too large to allow sufficient opportunity for competition. Consequently, the decision was taken to divide it into four separate operating companies: London Country North West, London Country South West, London Country North East and London Country South East (renamed Kentish Bus & Coach). Two further companies were formed to provide central services: Gatwick Engineering and Green Line Travel.

In 1988, all four operating companies were sold by NBC to four different purchasers and went their own separate ways, determining their own levels of Green Line provision. The two southern companies became somewhat disenchanted with the Green Line image and started to move away from the brand. London Country South West (subsequently renamed London & Country and later bought by Drawlane) took over several of the thriving airport services and put them in a separate company, Speedlink Airport Services (today owned by National Express Group and renamed 'Airlinks'), using the Speedlink and Jetlink branding.

As for Green Line, all four operating companies had a share in the company and contributed to its marketing and support-service

Db 3947

GREEN LINE COACHES, Ltd.

EXCHANGE TICKET

No. 21

London (Poland St. Coach Stn.)	Edenbridge (Star)
Streatham H. Theatre	Crockham Hl (Royal Oak)
Norbury Station	Oxted Station
Wst Croydon Station	Titsey Park Lodge
derstead Church	Worms Hth Cheverells Farm Gates
Chelsham Hare & H	A

Available to the Stage punched.

costs. However, it suffered from lack of leadership because no single shareholder company was in overall control.

Although the network was starting to shrink, Green Line managed to celebrate its 60th birthday (Diamond Jubilee) in 1990, but this was a modest affair compared with the 1980 Golden Jubilee. Many observers reckoned that Green Line's demise was imminent, and that there would be nothing further to celebrate. Deregulation of services outside London took its toll on Green Line through the withdrawal of the LT and county council subsidies which had been supporting several less-viable routes. Competition from the railways was beginning to increase, largely due to the vigorous marketing which followed the creation of Network SouthEast. Furthermore, the managers of the new companies which had shareholdings in Green Line Travel were too preoccupied with their own operational and financial affairs to bother much with the Green Line network. Subsequent changes in the ownership of the four companies frustrated the cohesion which was so greatly needed at this time.

Yet, Green Line is alive and kicking in the new Millennium, having experienced a gradual change of fortune over the latter years of the 1990s. The catalyst for this revival has been the increasing dominance of the Cowie Group (now renamed ARRIVA), the current owner of the Green Line name. Following a succession of complex takeovers, ARRIVA now has control, through its various subsidiaries, of over 80% of the original London Country operating area. The main 'missing piece' is approximately half of the former London Country North East operation, covering central Hertfordshire. This belongs to Sovereign, owned by Blazefield Holdings. Also, First Beeline has taken over the Slough and Windsor part of the old London Country empire.

Appreciating the significance of the historic and well-respected Green Line name, Green Line Travel has worked hard to promote the use of the brand by ARRIVA subsidiaries and third-party operators; indeed, an increasing number of coaches entering London, mainly tourist and commuter services, carry the current

► TPL89 belonged to a batch of Leyland Tigers built in 1985 which were of the longer variety (12m instead of 11m), with Plaxton Paramount 3200 bodywork. Previously in National Express livery, TPL89 was wearing Green Line colours when photographed in Queen Elizabeth Road, Kingston, in May 1991. *Geoff Rixon*

◂ For a time, prior to its repaint into striped Countryliner colours, this East Lancs-bodied Dennis Dominator worked Green Line services wearing a more subtle livery. The vehicle was photographed in April 1991 in London Road, Kingston with upstairs front passenger in relaxed pose. Built in 1988, F201 OPD later became DD1 in the fleet of ARRIVA Surrey & West Sussex (formerly London & Country) and was sold in 1998 to Bryn Melyn Motor Services of Llangollen. *Geoff Rixon*

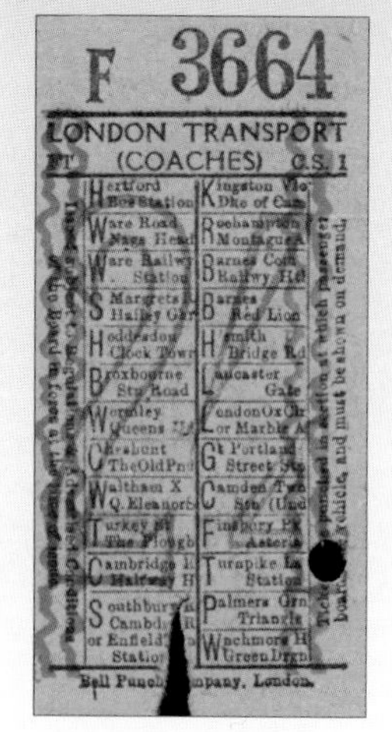

▲ The 726 version of the 725 southern orbital route, introduced on 21 May 1977 to serve Heathrow Airport, has had mixed fortunes over the years but still operates today, albeit not under the Green Line umbrella. For a time, it was withdrawn completely, but was reinstated by popular demand; as seen here, it has also been an LT service. This view shows TL8 at Hampton Court in August 1991 displaying the strapline 'Celebrating 60 Years of Service' beneath the fleetname, a hangover from the previous year. The garage code/running number bracket has recently been removed. *Geoff Rixon*

◂ To save the cost of buying new vehicles, London & Country undertook a programme of purchasing second-hand Leyland Nationals and having them rebuilt to Greenway specification by East Lancs. The programme ran from 1992 to 1995 and this view, west of Kingston Bridge, shows No 377, an ex-Alder Valley South vehicle dating from 1978. Delivered to London & Country in 1994, No 377 was subsequently re-registered PDZ 6277. At the time of this photograph, route 415, successor to the long-established 715, was an express service from Victoria for which Green Line branding had recently been reintroduced. The section from Kingston to Victoria was withdrawn in November 1997, and the remnant is now a red bus route. *Geoff Rixon*

Green Line livery dating back to the early 1990s, and the Green Line fleetname. Because the Green Line of today bears little resemblance to the old network and no longer serves many of the old familiar destinations (particularly in the south and south west, such as Tunbridge Wells, Crawley, Dorking and Reigate), some local people think that Green Line no longer exists. I tell them that, if they were to walk across Hungerford Bridge at Charing Cross in the morning rush hour, as I do, they would see large numbers of Green Line coaches ferrying commuters along the Victoria Embankment, as they did 70 years ago.

Indeed, in some respects, certain aspects of Green Line operation have not changed. The coaches still have a significant presence at Victoria, with a Green Line coach station in Bulleid Way, close to the previous Eccleston Bridge location. True, some unfamiliar fleetnames are now associated with Green Line. Maidstone & District started to use the name in 1995 for that network of London routes to the Medway towns and Maidstone which operated previously under the Invictaway banner (and is now confined to Maidstone, the Medway towns operation having passed to London Coaches (Kent) in May 1997). Southend Transport also started using the Green Line name in 1995. Other users include non-ARRIVA companies, eg Sovereign and First Beeline.

Some routes still carry familiar numbers in the 700 series, even though, in most cases, these are in fact different routes. Numbers 700/701/702 operate from London to Slough, Windsor and Bracknell; route 711 covers London to Redbridge and Harlow; route 718 is a summer operation from London to Hampton Court; route 724 still operates between Heathrow Airport, Watford, Hertford and Harlow; routes 748/758 link Hemel Hempstead with London; and routes 755 and 757 provide a service to London from Brent Cross and Luton Airport, plus commuter journeys

PDL202 (since renumbered 3442), one of nine low-floor DAF SB220s with Plaxton Prestige bodywork, belongs to ARRIVA East Herts & Essex. It is seen here on the well-known 724 route at Watford Junction on 15 August 1998. *Geoff Rixon*

from Luton and Dunstable. Then there is route 797, serving London, Hatfield, Stevenage and Baldock, having been cut back from Cambridge in November 1997. More recent developments are the increase in frequency of the 757 airport service to half-hourly, every day, and, from 10 October 1999, a joint service with First Thamesway under the Green Line banner from London to Canvey Island and Southend using numbers 720, 721, 722 and 723. Some other familiar services still operate, for example routes 726 and 740, but no longer under the Green Line brand.

It is significant that, when ARRIVA launched its new standard livery of aquamarine and stone in 1997, this was to be carried by all subsidiaries, replacing former company liveries and fleetnames. There was only one exception to this edict: Green Line. So now it is possible to see around 100 coaches operating in the Green Line livery of pale green (plus a certain Stagecoach RMC carrying full 1962 Green Line livery!). ARRIVA has recognised the goodwill attached to the famous Green Line name over its 70 years of existence. In the view of the travelling public, the various licensing authorities and other official bodies with which ARRIVA has to deal, Green Line is a familiar name which represents stability and high standards, in contrast with some of today's less well-established operators. The continuation of the Green Line name is now beginning to pay dividends, and hopefully the network will expand further over the coming years.

One thing is for sure: there cannot be many public-transport operators in London and the Home Counties with a fleetname which has lasted 70 years (or 66 years if you are a purist who takes into account the interregnum in the latter part of World War 2!). What is more, amid the general decline in bus and coach services, Green Line is showing signs of growth. Here's to the 75th Anniversary in 2005!

▲ On 29 July 1999, ARRIVA Southend No 553, looking well for a 15-year-old, negotiates Hyde Park Corner. This Leyland Tiger with Plaxton Paramount 3200 bodywork was previously TPL41 in the fleet of London Country South West. *Geoff Rixon*

Afterlife

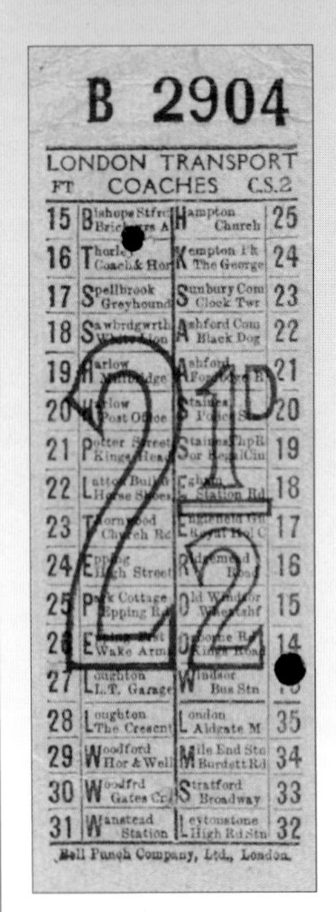

▶ Fortune failed to shine on T251 which disappeared into oblivion along with all but one of its second-series contemporaries and the entire first series of 7T7s. This sad scene was recorded at a farm in South Petherton, Somerset, on 19 March 1967.
Maurice Bateman

▲ Each of the main classes of prewar Green Line coach is represented in preservation, though in some cases more by luck than judgement. TF77 entered the LT Collection upon withdrawal, but Cobham Bus Museum inhabitant Q83, one of the temporary coach conversions, survived through being purchased from LT in 1954 by Sutton Coldfield Old People's Welfare Committee. This owner took great care of the vehicle and it was driven into preservation in 1966. Q83 and TF77 were photographed at Brent Cross while attending the Green Line Golden Jubilee rally in 1980. *Geoff Rixon*

Found by a fire engine enthusiast who spotted a familiar-looking roof protruding through dense undergrowth at Watling Street Motors' yard at Redbourne in Hertfordshire, T448 now sees the light of day once more in this March 1968 shot. The coach entered service at Hitchin in June 1936 and, after conversion to an ambulance during World War 2, was relegated to bus work in 1946. T448 was the last 9T9 in public service in Kingston; when its duties there ceased in 1952, it became a staff bus on the Reigate–Chiswick run. In March 1953, the vehicle was sold to Harperbury Hospital, St Albans, where it worked until suffering engine failure in 1958, going for scrap shortly after. This unique survivor, the only complete 9T9 known to exist, was restored at Cobham Bus Museum, near where the photograph on page 75 was taken in June 1983. Latterly, T448 has been off the road, but is now nearing the end of a major rebuild and will soon be operating at Cobham once again. *Maurice Bateman / Peter Plummer*

703
WROTHAM
via
London Victoria
GREEN LINE
703 WROTHAM LONDON AMERSHAM
KINGSDOWN FARNINGHAM LEWISHAM VICTORIA
703
ST
T448c
CXX 171
GREEN LINE
LONDON TRANSPORT

Restored 10T10 T504 has been a familiar sight at Cobham for many years, and it is easy to take its present resplendent condition for granted. Like T448, T504 was another chance discovery, this time at Chadderton, near Oldham, Lancashire, where it was spotted from the railway line. The coach entered service at Staines in May 1938, served as an ambulance during the war and returned to Green Line duties in 1946. In August 1951, it was sent to Kingston as a red bus to replace an aging 1T1 — none other than T31, one of its current stablemates at Cobham! Following withdrawal in May 1954, T504 passed through the hands of dealers before being bought for conversion to a mobile showroom. This plan did not materialise and it was sold in 1959 to the owner of the scrapyard seen here, owing its survival to the fact that it was intended for use as a mobile crane. T504, photographed as discovered in March 1968, was towed out of the yard on 28 December 1968, appropriately with Derek Parsons, who had been visited by T708 in Malaya (see page 27), taking the wheel. The later view of T504 was taken at Islington during the Anniversary Bus Parade on 8 July 1979, before the vehicle was re-fitted with its roofboard brackets. *Maurice Bateman / Geoff Rixon*

GREEN 702 LINE
GRAVESEND
VIA VICTORIA
T 504
ELP 228
GREEN LINE
X6M 981T

▲ This Duple-bodied second-series 7T7 entered service at Romford in January 1931, served as an ambulance during World War 2 and was the last of its class remaining in service when it was withdrawn from bus work in November 1950. One of the most important exhibits in the LT Collection and currently in working order, T219 is seen here at Clapham Common in May 1964, taking part in the annual Historic Commercial Vehicle Club run to Brighton. *Author*

T448 and T504 were amazing discoveries in the late 1960s, but who would imagine finding another prewar Green Line coach 30 years later in no worse condition than those? Max Hayles was delivering some saplings to a farm at Nyabing, some 319km south of Perth, Australia, in June 1997 when he discovered T499. Remarkably, it was largely complete apart from its front wheels, seats and destination boxes, still retaining its LT radiator badge and rear wheel discs. Bought from North's of Leeds (dealers) in 1954 by Tony Creasey for taking schoolchildren from Kendenup to Mt Barker (a round trip of about 25 miles per day) and resold in 1959 to Ted Collins for carrying out the same duties until 1962, T499 was so popular with the children because of its deep-cushioned seats that these were removed and fitted to its successor. T499 was purchased by John Thomson of Nyabing for conversion into a camper, but the project never reached fruition. On 24 November 1997, the vehicle was moved to a museum where, in the ownership of Ian Kerr and Graham Horton, it awaits restoration. *Max Hayles*

Coach Curiosities

The amazing LT1137: a graceful concave curve swept upwards from the lower-deck canopy to the upper-deck front windows; the roof had a raised central section containing a roll-back canvas hood. There was a front entrance but, strangely, a rear staircase, which meant that passengers desirous of the upstairs front seats had to walk two lengths of the vehicle! Ventilation for the upper deck, in addition to the roll-back hood, was obtained through scoops fitted alongside the raised section of the roof; ventilation for downstairs was through diagonal slots in the cantrail between the decks.
John Aldridge collection

In the early years of Green Line, several distinctive — if not extraordinary-looking — prototype coaches were developed. Although these were largely unsuccessful, they demonstrate the innovative thinking which was aimed at enhancing the Green Line image and capturing more passengers.

The first experimental vehicle appeared in 1931 and was intended as the forerunner of a fleet of double-deck coaches. Numbered LT1137, among a batch of single-deck chassis (and using one), this coach had a Chiswick-built body of striking external appearance, with luxurious seating. Unfortunately, LT1137 was not successful in coach service and was converted in 1935 into a bus. Withdrawal came in 1945 and this splendid-looking machine was broken up in September 1946.

The next oddity appeared in April 1933, although, by comparison with the other vehicles under review here, this was by far the least strange-looking. T232 was one of the second batch of AEC Regals with 30-seat front-entrance bodies, delivered between December 1930 and March 1931. The original body is believed to have been destroyed by fire, so the vehicle was sent to Weymann's at Addlestone, emerging with a distinctive metal-framed body built to Metropolitan-Cammell design.

Although some value may have been derived from T232 as a guinea-pig for future metal-framed bodies fitted by Weymann to old T-type chassis — including, ironically, T232 itself — the vehicle lasted only five years in Green Line (and, indeed, LT) service in this form. The body was then mounted on R4, an AEC Reliance, which was sold in October 1938. The chassis, with a replacement metal body from a Reliance, remained in service until 1952, when it was broken up by LT.

At this point, mention should be made of two experimental side-engined Qs which had Green Line connections. The first, Q1, was a single-deck bus which was used for a short time on Green Line services at Reigate during 1933. The vehicle was the prototype of the class which subsequently provided 77 Green Line coaches. The second, Q188, was a double-decker coach finished in Green Line livery but apparently only ever used on bus work. This vehicle was a natural successor to LT1137, representing a further attempt to create a prototype for a purpose-built fleet of double-deck coaches. Seating 51 passengers, Q188 entered stock in February 1937, and was intended for the Romford

◀ LT1137 entered service at Reigate garage on 22 September 1931 on route E which ran between Redhill and Bushey. Following withdrawal of this route in October 1933, it was transferred to routes I and J, operating from Leavesden Road (Watford) garage for its remaining 18 months or so of Green Line service. This photograph was taken at Oxford Circus in October 1931. *John Aldridge collection*

Green Line services. Alas, it remained unlicensed for 15 months before being sent to Hertford to work alongside four double-deck Qs on local bus services.

While LT was working on the Green Line double-deck Q design, it was also collaborating with Leyland Motors on a radical concept for a new single-deck Green Line coach. This would be the forerunner of the highly-successful TF class. The prototype, TF1, differed fundamentally from the later production models by having an ugly glass cab, which was rebuilt to a more orthodox design in 1940. The vehicle was delivered to LT by Leyland Motors on 10 July 1937 and entered service on 1 December 1937 at Tunbridge Wells for use on routes C1 and C2. It was sold to an independent coach operator in 1946.

With the reinstatement of Green Line services after the war, LT turned its thoughts yet again to the concept of a purpose-built fleet of double-deck coaches. Following bomb damage, RT97 had been rebuilt in 1946 for a Pay-as-you-Board (PAYB) experiment which involved the conductor's sitting beside newly-installed platform doors, collecting fares. On 18 April 1946, RT97 was sent to Romford for trials on Green Line duties, but long queues built up due to the limited number of passengers that could be accommodated on the platform while waiting to pay. The vehicle was subsequently adapted for conventional mobile-conductor operation and proved popular with passengers, continuing in Green Line service until 5 January 1947.

In the meantime, desperate to place higher-capacity vehicles (ie double-deckers) on the busy Romford routes out of Aldgate, and undeterred by the failure of LT1137 and Q188, LT sought authority for another prototype double-decker coach. However, shortages of labour and materials made construction of a new vehicle out of the question, so LT decided on a compromise: the reconstruction of RT97.

The RT coach, numbered RTC1, was completed in January 1949 and entered Green Line service in April 1949. Unfortunately, the vehicle was fundamentally flawed. Problems included mechanical unreliability (RTC1 still had RT97's old engine, albeit modified), spongy suspension and a tendency for the saloon to overheat. After only nine months' coach operation, RTC1 was down-graded to bus duty and was sold by LT in March 1953 for eventual use as staff transport by Vernon's, the football pools promoter. It was scrapped in the 1960s.

The result of the RTC1 fiasco was that LT decided to use standard RT double-deckers for the Romford routes. Yet LT was determined to achieve its goal of operating a successful double-deck coach and, after 26 years of trying, was blessed with the magnificent CRL4, the prototype Routemaster coach which lasted an amazing 22 years in regular service, albeit latterly as a bus.

The attractive interior of T232; note the raised seats over and behind the wheels — a design perpetuated in the 9T9s and 10T10s, and which offered rear seat passengers much-improved vision.
John Aldridge collection

◂ T232's new all-metal body was completed and fitted to the chassis in April 1933, as seen in these photographs. Despite the overall appearance being somewhat ponderous, the vehicle had sweeping lines, created by the extension of the polished-metal horizontal mouldings and black waistband around the part of the body in which the raised seats were fitted. Unusually, the rear bumpers and side guardrails were fitted to the chassis frame and not to the bodywork, but the most note-worthy external feature was undoubtedly the illuminated route-points, inset above the first few windows on each side (and incomplete, in the nearside view shown here). However, although this feature was popular with some operators, it was clearly too radical for Green Line, because, before long, the panels were filled in and the traditional wooden roofboards fitted.
John Aldridge collection

The Leyland Tiger FEC (flat-engined coach) became the TF class in LT service. The positioning of the side-mounted 8.6-litre engine is clearly visible in this shot of the prototype, TF1, under construction at Leyland's factory on 7 May 1937. The interior and front views were taken on 13 July 1937. TF1 differed from the production models in having a grotesque-looking glass cab and single rear wheels. The cab, which the driver entered from the saloon, projected outwards and provided excellent all-round visibility. The driver's seat was some 18in higher than normal, apparently enabling the driver to see the road to within 6in of the front of the coach. *John Aldridge collection*

▲ The photograph on this page shows TF1 with its rebuilt driver's cab dating from 1940. The vehicle, being non-standard, was sold prematurely in 1946 and purchased by Castle Coaches of Lewisham. *Geoff Rixon*

▲ RTC1, the one and only 'real' RT coach, bore no resemblance to its original incarnation as RT97, apart from the rear dome and upper-deck emergency window. The front end was completely redesigned with a sloping bonnet, which required the removal of the radiator to a position beneath the staircase. The side windows were altered to give a panoramic impression, created by fitting very slender, aluminium-faced pillars between the windows and removing the half-drop cross-bars. Inside, air-conditioning and fluorescent lighting, both in their infancy, were installed. Like RT97, platform doors were fitted. RTC1 lasted only nine months on Green Line duties after which, from the beginning of 1950 until itswithdrawal in March 1953, it operated from Leatherhead garage on the one-vehicle 416 service. It is seen here at Esher on 26 July 1952. *C. Carter*

From Tamplin & Makovski to ARRIVA: The Reigate Connection

The Surrey market town of Reigate has played a dominant role throughout most of Green Line's existence. Yet, had it not been for the foresight and determination of one of its residents, a certain Arthur Henry Hawkins, the history of London country bus and coach operation might well have taken a totally different course.

Arthur Hawkins was born in the adjacent town of Redhill in 1881, and left school at the age of 15. Starting work at a grocer's and then becoming a rent collector, he joined a firm of electrical engineers, Tamplin & Makovski, based at 57 Bell Street, Reigate, when he was 17. His work enabled him to travel around, and he became aware of the growth and apparent success of motorbus operations in surrounding areas. This contrasted with the position in Reigate, where horsebuses still held sway and two attempts to run motorbuses between Reigate and Redhill in 1905-6 and again in 1909 had foundered, due to the unreliability of vehicles and inexperience of operators. Mr Hawkins saw an opportunity here and, in order not to alert possible competitors, wrote to a transport journal seeking advice on the operation of a specific motorbus service without revealing the intended route (Reigate to Redhill). In the light of the encouraging reply published in the magazine, Mr Hawkins decided to proceed and sought further advice, as well as turning to his employers for support. With a local brewer, J. W. Neale, as Chairman, A. W. Makovski as a Director and Mr Hawkins as Company Secretary (part-time), the East Surrey Traction Co was formed on 16 March 1911, and two 30hp Leyland buses were obtained on hire purchase. The route commenced on 23 May 1911, operating from Tamplin & Makovski's premises.

The service was an instant success and, in the following month, Mr Hawkins joined the company on a full-time basis, and a third bus was obtained. With the arrival of three more vehicles in January 1912 for the extension to Merstham and Earlswood, new garage and office premises were required and these were built at 75 Bell Street, just along from Tamplin & Makovski's. The adjacent pair of houses was also acquired, but not yet used by the company. These dwellings stood on the corner of Bell Street and Lesbourne Road. The garage was extended in 1914 to house 12 buses, and again in 1920 to accommodate 36 buses, as well as the motor car retailing and repair business purchased by East Surrey from Tamplin & Makovski in the previous year.

This close-up of the front of an East Surrey touring coach was taken at the new Reigate garage in December 1931. The vehicle was from a batch of 10 AEC Regals with open-roof bodywork (C30F) by Hall Lewis (later to become Park Royal). These coaches entered service in March 1931 and were transferred to the Green Line fleet in May 1932, at which point the East Surrey fleetname on the canopy (as shown in the picture) changed to the Green Line name (see T320 on pages 88-9). LCGS numbered these vehicles T315-324, oblivious the fact that LGOC had allocated the numbers T307-318 to 12 ex-Thomas Tilling AEC Regal buses. The duplication was discovered when the Country Area records of LPTB were transferred to Chiswick in 1935, whereupon Green Line coaches T307-318 were renumbered T391-402.
John Aldridge collection

East Surrey had no significant competition at the outset, but Mr Hawkins was alarmed when the powerful London General Omnibus Co (LGOC) started a Sunday service in July 1913 from Stockwell to Redhill, penetrating the company's area. The LGOC had failed to obtain licences from Reigate Council and, when Mr Hawkins complained, was forced to pull back to Merstham.

As a result of this initial skirmish, Mr Hawkins was not favourably disposed towards the LGOC. Consequently, when he was planning to buy some Leyland double-deckers and Daimler got to hear and made overtures to him, he rebuffed the approach

Reigate garage occupied a 1.2-acre site and cost £30,000 to build. The structure, the work of Wallis, Gilbert & Partners, was of remarkable design, due to Reigate Council's concern about the visual impact of a typical utilitarian bus garage on the view from the town across Churchfields. The rear aspect, bordering the fields, was designed in half-timbered style, with a steep roof and a small tower topped by a weather vane. The front of the garage facing Lesbourne Road also had a steep, tiled roof. These features concealed six ridged-metal-and-glass roofs recessed between the elevations. The roofs were supported by lattice girders some 250ft long which eliminated the need for any internal pillars and enabled 170 vehicles to be accommodated. *John Aldridge collection*

The huge interior of the new Reigate garage presents an interesting array of vehicles in this August 1932 view. On the left is T246, a Weymann-bodied second-series 7T7 which was converted into a 6½-ton towing lorry (No 400W) in June 1939, and lasted in the departmental fleet until April 1960. Alongside is T320, an East Surrey private-hire coach with folding roof and Hall Lewis bodywork, being used here as a Green Line relief. In 1938 T320 was converted into a trolleybus-lubricating van (No 114W) and was withdrawn in May 1959. Two of T320's contemporaries, including T322, stand to the right of the second suspended chain, and to their right are two canvas-roofed R-type Reliance coaches, as used on LGOC's inaugural coach service in 1929 before the T-types arrived. Behind the second chain is a first-series 7T7 (with raised Green Line indicator box), and to the left of that are three of East Surrey's fleet of six canvas-roofed ADC 419s, which were used for Green Line work until 1933. *John Aldridge collection*

REDHILL
LONDON
REIGATE
PRIVATE
PRIVATE

The front of Reigate garage in July 1934, showing the offices, which accompanied the garage, on the left. The rear of the offices was also built in Old English style, and still looks very smart today. T246, from the first series of 7T7s, is setting off for Watford. The coach was sold in December 1938 and its original Hall Lewis body replaced.
John Aldridge collection

▲ because the Daimler chassis was assembled by AEC which belonged to the Underground group, owner of LGOC. However, Daimler persisted and Mr Hawkins accepted an invitation to attend its offices. There, he was introduced to W. J. Iden, Manager of LGOC, and this led to a meeting with Albert Stanley, head of the Underground group, and, subsequently, with Frank Pick, his deputy. They gave him an assurance that LGOC did not intend to run competitive services on East Surrey routes but merely wished to run Sunday excursions to Redhill and Reigate. With that, Mr Hawkins lent his support to LGOC's application to Reigate Council for the necessary licences.

This change of heart by Mr Hawkins was a shrewd move because it led to co-operation rather than confrontation with East Surrey's huge neighbour, starting a relationship which would eventually give him control of the Green Line coach operation when it was formed 17 years later. The first stage of this alliance was the signing of an agreement on 26 January 1914 defining the areas of each company's operations and committing East Surrey to buying Daimlers.

By now, East Surrey was going from strength to strength, enlarging its fleet and extending its services. However, the start of World War 1 put paid to any further expansion plans, and Mr Hawkins had to turn to LGOC for vehicles to cover shortages arising from wartime restrictions on bus production.

Once the war ended in November 1918, East Surrey started expanding its operations once more, and formed an even closer relationship with LGOC. In November 1919, Mr Hawkins expressed his concerns to Frank Pick about the risk of competition in the northern part of Surrey and suggested that East Surrey should develop this area on behalf of LGOC, with the latter loaning buses and providing the capital for new garages. LGOC liked the idea but had no spare buses at the time; eventually, however, the plan went ahead. On 7 July 1921, Mr Makovski and Mr Hawkins, who was by now Managing Director of East Surrey, signed a new contract to replace the area agreement which had officially expired in 1919. East Surrey was now operating agent for LGOC in a defined area to the south and south east of London, outside the Metropolitan Police district. LGOC agreed to supply the vehicles and garages to enable East Surrey to fulfil its obligations, although East Surrey was still responsible for meeting its operational needs from its own resources in those areas outside LGOC boundaries. Reigate was still the only garage and was

▲ Vehicles under repair at Reigate in July 1934 (see page 12) include ST1105 with RSJ body, private-hire coach T316 and first-series 7T7 T132. The latter was exported to Germany in 1945.
John Aldridge collection

During the 1950s, before the LT Museum Collection was put on public display, firstly at Clapham, then Syon Park and now Covent Garden/Acton, Reigate garage was the home of these historic vehicles. Sandwiched between a service RT and a preserved tram are CR14, TF77, Q55 and T219, the second and fourth vehicles being former Green Line coaches. *John Aldridge*

▲ leased, but East Surrey was able to secure its position through buying the freehold and that of the two adjacent houses. The company also started a garage-building programme in Surrey and Kent to provide permanent accommodation for its growing fleet, which in 1923 consisted of 39 company-owned buses and charabancs, and 64 buses loaned by LGOC. In the previous year, as if to reinforce its relationship with LGOC, East Surrey had changed its vehicle livery from blue to red.

As a result of the association with LGOC, East Surrey's fleet consisted mainly of AECs, and in September 1925 East Surrey was appointed an official AEC agent, augmenting its existing motor car agency business. The LGOC link was further strengthened in 1927 when LGOC acquired Surrey Hills Motor Services from Aldershot & District, handing operations over to East Surrey, and in 1928, with the acquisition of Autocar, the Tunbridge Wells-based operator, Mr Hawkins and Mr Makovski were appointed to the Autocar board.

Despite the close relationship between LGOC and East Surrey, LGOC was concerned that East Surrey might fall into the hands of a predator such as the Southern Railway. LGOC therefore decided to purchase the shares of East Surrey, which became a subsidiary of LGOC on 12 June 1929. Mr Neale and Mr Makovski resigned from the East Surrey board but Mr Hawkins continued as Managing Director and was given considerable autonomy. Indeed, to the outside world, the takeover was scarcely noticeable.

In August 1928, East Surrey had introduced an express coach service from Reigate to Charing Cross, although this lasted for less than nine months, due to insufficient patronage. Nevertheless, during 1929 the concept of express coach services running into London from some 30 to 35 miles out was gaining momentum, and LGOC ordered 100 new T-class coaches to compete in this growing market. Twelve of these coaches went to East Surrey for the restart of operations from

▲ Route 711 was withdrawn on 1 October 1977. Here at Reigate, LNC53 keeps company with two red staff buses, RF486 and RF471, the latter eventually working on the last day of RF public service, 30 March 1979. *John Aldridge*

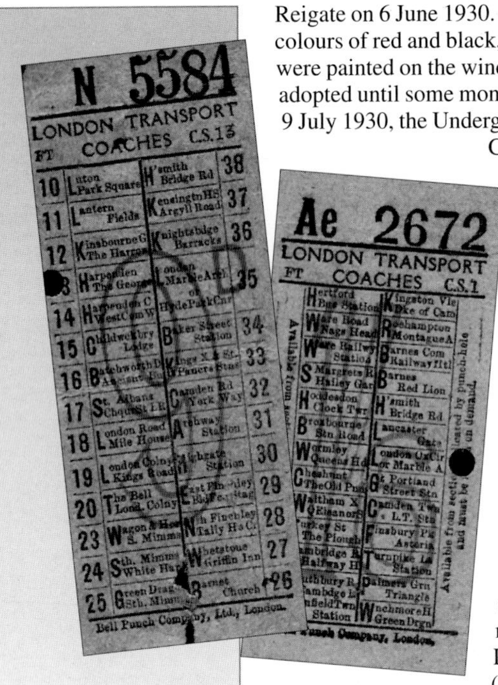

Reigate on 6 June 1930. The vehicles carried LGOC coach colours of red and black, with grey roofs, and the place-names were painted on the window louvres (roofboards were not adopted until some months on). Just over a month later, on 9 July 1930, the Underground group formed Green Line Coaches Ltd, and Arthur Hawkins, who is widely credited with having invented the name, was appointed Operating Manager. The vehicles were soon carrying the new green and black livery and, with Mr Hawkins at the helm, the Green Line coach network grew rapidly.

In 1932, LGOC handed over to East Surrey those services to the north of London which the National Omnibus Transport Co Ltd had previously operated on an agency basis for LGOC in the same way as East Surrey had operated in the south. East Surrey now became a misnomer, given the new operation on the other side of London, and so the company's name was changed in January 1932 to London General Country Services Ltd (LGCS). The headquarters of LGCS remained at Bell Street, Reigate, and Arthur Hawkins continued as Managing Director.

The change of company name coincided with the opening of a new garage and offices in Lesbourne Road, Reigate, behind the Bell Street premises. The stage was now set for expanding Reigate's role. The new garage assumed responsibility for the overhaul of all ex-East Surrey, Autocar and Green Line buses and coaches. In April 1932, the headquarters of Green Line Coaches was moved from 55 Broadway to Reigate, and on 27 July 1932 the Green Line business was officially transferred to LGCS.

LGCS's reign turned out to be short-lived, because on 1 July 1933 the London Passenger Transport Board (LPTB), using the name 'London Transport' (LT), acquired all the operating companies of the Underground group, including LGOC, LGCS and Green Line. The Country Bus & Coach Department, as it became known, which subsumed Green Line, continued to be based at Reigate, and Mr Hawkins was appointed General Manager. However, on 25 February 1935, vehicle overhauls were transferred from Reigate to Chiswick Works.

During World War 2, vehicle overhauls returned to Reigate as Chiswick switched to aircraft production. In the latter stages of the war, Mr Hawkins, who was still occupying the post of General Manager, Country Buses & Coaches, started planning the resumption of Green Line services, which had been suspended since 1943. On 1 March 1946, Arthur Henry Hawkins, JP, MInstT, retired from LT at the age of 65 after 35 years of bus and coach involvement at Reigate — a remarkable achievement. Over that period, the fleet under his control had expanded from two to over 1,000 vehicles. Mr Hawkins died at his Reigate home on 23 April 1963, aged 82.

Although control of Country buses and Green Line coaches did not stay continuously at Reigate after LT's creation in 1933, when it returned in 1967 it was there to stay, because Reigate became the headquarters of the newly-formed London Country Bus Services Ltd (LCBS) which took over LT's Country Bus & Coach operations on 1 January 1970. Indeed, Reigate regained its former strategic importance and LCBS added an extension to the 1932-built offices. This opened in March 1972, whereupon

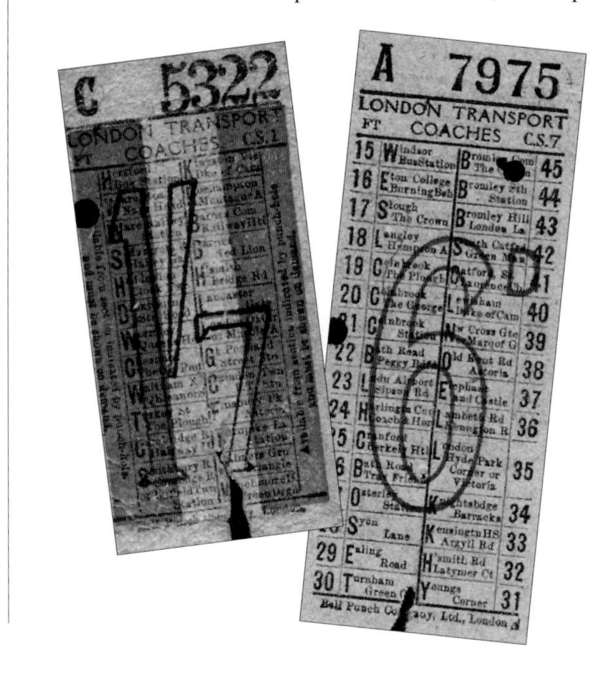

LCBS was able to put its entire headquarters, part of which had been outhoused, under one roof.

Sadly, Reigate's heyday was to be relatively short-lived.

In the fast-moving world of bus deregulation and privatisation during the 1980s, LCBS was split into four separate companies and these were sold off in 1988 to different purchasers. Most of the large headquarters at Reigate was no longer required but the garage remained in use by the local company, London & Country, until it became surplus to requirements. Its doors closed for the last time on 14 April 1996, a few months before British Bus, owner of London & Country, was bought by Cowie (now called ARRIVA). Green Line Travel, formed when LCBS was divided, continued to occupy part of the former East Surrey offices until January 1998.

So, as we enter the new millennium, what is left of the Reigate that played such a significant part in the history of country bus and coach services? The Bell Street site formerly occupied by Tamplin & Makovski was redeveloped in the 1930s, and No 57 is now an Indian restaurant. The old garage and corner-site houses (the former offices) lasted until quite recently, but have now been replaced by new buildings. The 1932-built offices look to be in good shape and are now called Linden Court (the 1972 extension is known as Chatham Court). But the magnificent garage has all but vanished. The building was Grade II listed, but English Heritage has agreed to the construction of a three-storey office block, subject to the retention of the half-timbered rear façades and the extreme western corner of the front, including the old vehicle entrance. This retained portion will be used for restaurant purposes. Luckily the new offices will be subject to a height restriction, intended to prevent the building from rising above the retained rear walls. Thus the traditional view across Churchfields should remain unchanged, although the back of the garage has long been screened by mature trees. It is naturally sad that so little of the original building has been saved, but apparently it proved impossible to find an appropriate use for the structure, and the new development, to be known as the Omnibus Building, at least ensures preservation of a small part of this unique garage. Work is already underway, and the end result should prove most interesting. Whether the tower and the splendid weather-vane with its silhouette of a coach find a home as part of the new building will remain to be seen but encouragingly, the structure is still on site, sitting on the ground.

Finally, despite the loss of bus garage facilities at Reigate, Green Line is still in Reigate at the time of writing (July 2000) even though none of its coaches frequents the town. This is the location of the expanding helpline' telephone-enquiry office serving Green Line and providing information on behalf of county councils, various ARRIVA subsidiaries and other bus and coach operators. So the Reigate connection is still intact, but sadly, will not be by the time this book is published. Problems over expansion at its Croydon Road premises mean that Green Line Travel has to move half a mile outside the Reigate post town boundary to Endsleigh Road, South Merstham, which is part of Redhill but still close to Green Line's traditional home.